Romans

Romans

The Definitive RogueCleric Commentary Using Tools of Hebrew Rhetoric

ROBERT B. McLEOD

WIPF & STOCK · Eugene, Oregon

ROMANS
The Definitive RogueCleric Commentary Using Tools of Hebrew Rhetoric

Wipf & Stock
An Imprint of Wipf and Stock Publishers
199 W. 8th Ave., Suite 3
Eugene, OR 97401

www.wipfandstock.com

PAPERBACK ISBN: 978-1-7252-7393-1
HARDCOVER ISBN: 978-1-7252-7394-8
EBOOK ISBN: 978-1-7252-7395-5

07/28/25

This commentary is dedicated to all those who have suffered from bad soteriology. God has not forgotten you.

"But God does not take away life; instead, he devises ways so that a banished person may not remain estranged from him."
2 Samuel 14:14b. (NIV)

The Rogue Cleric

Contents

List of Tables ix
Acknowledgments xi
Introduction xiii
Chapter 1 1
Chapter 2 16
Chapter 3 23
Chapter 4 31
Chapter 5 38
Chapter 6 50
Chapter 7 57
Chapter 8 63
Chapter 9 74
Chapter 10 86
Chapter 11 94
Chapter 12 105
Chapter 13 118
Chapter 14 126
Chapter 15 134
Chapter 16 145
Glossary of Soteriological Terms 153
Bibliography 159

List of Tables

Table 1: How We Are Justified 43
Table 2: How We Can Be Saved 44
Table 3: Christian Faith and Practice 45

Acknowledgments

First and foremost, I would like to acknowledge the excellent work done by Robert Arthur Bailey in translating Paul's Letter to the Romans from the Greek and arraying it in a way that illustrates Paul's use of Hebraic rhetorical tools. His fine work, from which I deviate only occasionally, made this commentary possible. He has graciously allowed me to reprint his translation, with footnotes, in full. His translation is available on the very fine website *InTheBeginning.org*. This text was laboriously and beautifully transferred from PDF format to Word by my editor, Martha Kretschmer. Her contributions to the final appearance of the work cannot be overemphasized.

Secondly, I would like to acknowledge my debt to Kenneth Bailey, no relation to Robert, for his pioneering work in the area of New Testament exegesis referencing Hebrew rhetoric. Kenneth immersed himself in Middle Eastern culture, learning Arabic "without an accent," and learning to think like an Easterner as opposed to a Greek. I urged him to write his own commentary on the entire New Testament, but failing in that request, I have undertaken to do for Romans what I wish he had done himself. His work would no doubt have been superior.

Finally, I would like to acknowledge my debt to the Church Pension Fund of the Episcopal Church, whose disability and retirement benefits have given me the time to theologize and write this commentary. I have not been idle.

Introduction

This commentary is neither comprehensive nor exhaustive. It is meant to serve as an emendation and corrective to what others have written. I am a great admirer of D. Martyn Lloyd-Jones's six-volume commentary on Romans 3:20 to 8:39, the portion of the letter he felt was paramount. He left chapter 9 untouched, however, which is a shame. Martin Luther made extensive reference to Romans, saying in his preface to his German translation, "This letter is truly the most important piece in the New Testament. It is purest Gospel. It is well worth a Christian's while not only to memorize it word for word but also to occupy himself with it daily, as though it were the daily bread of the soul. It is impossible to read or to meditate on this letter too much or too well."[1] He traces his theological conversion to contemplating verse 1:17, and John Wesley came to personal faith while listening to a sermon that quoted Luther's preface.

Romans is Paul's most self-consciously theological letter. Typically, his letters focused on pastoral issues generated by the struggle of living a Christian life in a pagan world. Romans has its share of pastoral admonitions, but from the outset, Paul is looking for opportunities to depart from the immediate to focus instead on the eternal, to use the pastoral as a springboard to address the theological. Once the theological foundation has been laid, he can return to the pastoral. For him, doctrine leads to understanding, understanding leads to hope, and hope leads to godliness.

Paul's theological concerns revolved around what he calls the *mystery of God*, namely, how a humanity divided into Jew and Gentile could be reconciled to God and each other that they all might become one. His audience in Rome is predominately Gentile but nevertheless includes prominent Jewish members. Paul is therefore faced with the challenge of introducing concepts that may be novel to one group or the other, without losing touch with either one. Even though Paul was eminently successful in achieving

1. Luther, *Preface*, lines 1–2.

balance in his presentation, we in the West have been relatively unsophisticated in our interpretation of the text.

I maintain that all our theological conundrums are caused by reading a Jewish or Eastern document, the Bible, with a Western or Greek mindset. While this is a problem when reading the rest of the Bible, it becomes critical when reading Romans. It's not that Paul showed his own cultural limitations by thinking and writing like a Jew, but that as a Jew he was in possession of concepts and insights that cannot be translated into an Aristotelian idiom without alteration and loss. As will become clear in my exposition, there is a reason God chose one people as his medium of specific revelation: a long history of interaction with God has given the Jews a unique spiritual and intellectual heritage. We have to read and think like them if we want to understand that revelation. We in the West have let our cultural and intellectual prejudices obscure the fine balance Paul worked so hard to achieve.

Let me be specific. To really understand Paul, you have to remember that as a Pharisee, he used the rhetorical tools most favored by rabbis in their scholarship and disputations. Chief among these tools is that of symmetrical parallelism, or chiastic structure. Instead of a linear sequence of syllogistic deduction, as Greeks tended to favor, the Hebrew rabbis, Jesus included, would construct an argument that makes a series of points, each following from that which precedes it. They reach a conclusion, and then the argument is repeated in reverse order until they return to the starting point. Thus, the points in a seven-step chiasmus could be viewed as ABCDCBA. Each intermediate step shares a similar thought with its corresponding step. Sometimes these thoughts are simple repetition, sometimes the second is a corollary to the first. This device can be found in a single sentence, a paragraph, or even the whole document. It was used to show the inherent logic of the statements being made; to provide clarity in a written medium that lacked spaces, sentences, paragraphs, capitalization, punctuation, or other delimiters; and to aid in memorization where written documents were the exception rather than the rule. As we will see, to read a chiasmus as linear thought can lead to confusion and genuine suffering.

Another tendency is for Paul to express himself in the form of a diatribe—that is, an informal rhetorical dialogue with imaginary opponents. Sometimes he labels his antagonists, "Now you, if you call yourself a Jew," but he's usually content to refer to his audience in abstract terms that render his attacks less threatening. The translation introduces labels that help clarify this back and forth repartee: *Paul*, *Jewish Teacher*, or *Teacher of Law*. Further, Paul employs litotes, where he uses double negatives to assert a positive.

Finally, in addition to what Paul did, we should pay attention to what he did not do. He avoids terms that would tend to defeat his intention of bringing reconciliation to a mixed congregation of both Jew and Gentile. For instance, he avoids the term *church* in the opening address. Nor does he speak of Christians, for he doesn't want to act as though Judaism is totally bankrupt and being replaced. Further, he avoids speaking of synagogues because they have historically been the province of Jews alone. He knows God is making a new humanity in Christ, and he avoids using terms that hearken back to old distinctions. Instead, he speaks of family and the unity implied by that concept. His overarching theme is that we can all join God's family, where he's a benevolent father who has met all our needs in the person of his son. He speaks variously to Gentiles, then Jews, then back again repeatedly. He's always mindful of the criticisms his ideas will arouse, and he's careful to deal with each in its turn. Every once in a while, he's able to drop his defenses and sing a hymn of praise to God without reservation.

In order to display the rhetorical structure of this epistle, I've used Robert Bailey's translation of the Greek text,[2] the *Novum Testamentum Graece*.[3] The Scripture is laid out in cascading format to illustrate the chiastic form as perceived by its modern translator, in an attempt to reconstruct what Paul originally intended. Words in italics indicate text not found in the Greek source. The Bailey translation precedes my comments. Robert Bailey and I both provide footnotes for further clarification and commentary—his are primarily concerned with rhetorical structure, mine with exegetical interpretation. His notes appear immediately following the scripture excerpts, while mine follow normal footnote patterns. My footnotes are intended to complement his. The New International Version of the Bible is by necessity a paraphrase, edited in order to read better and offer more clarity. When it provides something the Bailey text misses, I have added it with notation. In addition to using italics for emphasis, words in my comments that are italicized are keywords pulled from the scripture passage. Words that are capitalized in the body of a sentence should be understood as referring to cardinal concepts or typologies.

2. Bailey, "God's Good News to the Romans."

3. Nestle et al., *Novum Testamentum Graece*.

The overall structure of the letter forms a chiasmus along the lines of ABCBA:

A) 1:1–7
B) 1:8–17
C) 1:18—15:13
B) 15:14—16:23
A) 16:25–27

Thus, A and B consist of greetings, housekeeping preliminaries, and buttoning up. The main body of the text, C, consists of insights into God's plan of redemption that has revolutionized the standing of all humanity, Jew and Gentile, in his eyes. This main body, which is extensive, can be further subdivided as a chiasmus along the lines of ABCCBA:

A) 1:18—3:20: Jews and Gentiles have both dishonored God.
B) 3:21—4:25: Jews and Gentiles alike can receive righteousness from God.*
C) 5:1—8:39: All are justified, those who live by the Spirit are also saved.*
C) 9:1—11:36: God's plan of redemption as experienced by Jew and Gentile.*
B) 12:1—13:14: Life in the Spirit within the church and society.*
A) 14:1—15:13: Potential cultural conflicts between Jew and Gentile.*

* I have renamed all sections except the first and have included these titles in the chapter introductions. Bailey's original titles are included with the text of the scripture.

It is interesting to note that the major exegetical blunders that have been committed by interpreters of this epistle have occurred in the two sections of conclusion labeled C above. In the case of Romans 5, we have no commentators to my knowledge who make a distinction between justification and salvation, as Paul does. Like Calvin, they assume this is simple parallelism or repetition, not a profound distinction that clarifies the rest of Christian soteriology.[4] In 8:29–30, my exposition shows that a linear interpretation leads to misunderstanding, while a chiastic interpretation leads to clarity and logic. In this way I'm able to offer a reconstituted *Ordo Salutis*, a genuine first. In the case of Romans 9, most commentators, including Calvin and Luther, adopt a literalistic approach as opposed to metaphorical.

4. Will Durant says of Calvin, "... we shall always find it hard to love the man who darkened the human soul with the most absurd and blasphemous conception of God in all the long and honored history of nonsense." Durant, *The Reformation*, 490.

The result, especially for Calvin, is an atrocious image of God who hates his creation.[5] Time and again in these critical sections, chiastic structures play an important part in conveying the sense of Paul's argument. These and other themes are repeated whenever warranted by the text.

Chapter designations in the Bible are arbitrary at best, but they serve to divide the text and commentary into manageable portions. For ease, my chapters correspond with the text of Romans. Because theologians do not always use words in the same way, I've appended a Glossary of Soteriological Terms at the end of the commentary to document how I understand these words. I believe I am using them in the sense Paul was. Let us keep Paul's goals and methods in mind as we read the text and confront those passages that have led to the doctrinal and denominational confusion that characterizes the Christian church today. We should read Paul according to his methods and intentions, not our own.

5. Frederick Calder writes of Calvin's view of God: "... as a being of whom, in point of malignity, the prince of the lower regions is but a faint image and expression. ... far more odious than anything ever dictated by the prophet of Mecca." Calder, *Memoirs of Simon Episcopius*, 267–68.

Chapter 1

PRÉCIS

The first chapter of Romans can best be understood as stretching across three rhetorical structures in the mind of its author. Paul wrote according to his habits and intent, and the subsequent chapter divisions straddled the original outline and obscured its form. As mentioned in the Introduction, 1:1–7 constitutes A, the first part of a global chiasmus, which bookends with 16:25–27. This first section is an address, a summary of the Good News, and a blessing, and it is a minor chiasmus of its own. The second section, 1:8–17, is also a minor chiasmus. This section gives thanks for the Romans' faithfulness and speaks of Paul's prayers and plans. Starting at 1:18 and going to the end of the chapter, we have a litany of sins against God, starting with Gentiles. Of note in this last portion is a rehearsal of how wrong worship leads to wrong thinking and wrong thinking leads to wrong behavior. This sequence of decadence reflects Paul's understanding that we are three-part creatures: if the Spirit doesn't dominate, the body will, and the slavish mind will follow.

Address, summary of the good news, blessing1

1 Paul, a slave of **Anointed Jesus**,
called *to be* an apostle,
set apart for God's good news,
2 which he promised before through his prophets in *the* holy
scriptures 3 concerning his son,
who was born by David's seed
according to flesh,
4 who was appointed God's Son In Power

according to spirit of holiness
by resurrection of *the* dead,
Jesus Anointed our Lord,
5 through whom
we have received grace and apostleship
for obedience of faithfulness in all nations
for his name's sake,
6 among whom are you also, Jesus Anointed's called *ones*,
7 To all who are in Rome,
God's loved *ones*,
called *to be* holy *ones*:
Grace to you and peace from God our Father and the **Lord Jesus Anointed.**

[1] 1:1–7 The first of five divisions of this letter. Parallel with 16:25–27. Paul's longest opening address.

Although the first seven verses constitute a chiasmus, I will deal with the verses sequentially, as they contain many important terms that require definition. Note, however, the symmetry of the opening address with its emphasis on God's call upon the Roman congregation.

V. 1

The letter was written by Paul. He hadn't been to Rome, but as with other citizens in the Roman world, life was not complete without a visit to the capital. A congregation had been established there by other Christians, and there was apparent friction between Jew and Gentile about the degree to which Christians had to adopt Jewish customs with regard to circumcision and dietary practices. This conflict was universal in the emerging Christian church and became the subject of the first ecumenical council in Jerusalem around AD 49. The problem is addressed not only by Paul, but also Peter and, by implication, the apostle John in his Revelation. The controversy led to mutual antagonism and distrust between Jew and Gentile, and so Paul seeks to diffuse the problem by getting at the root issue. Until we know how a holy God intends to redeem a sinful humanity, we can't know how we should respond. What has God done that we cannot do? What is God looking for by way of response? How do we live a life pleasing to God, and how do we offend him and endanger our spiritual standing? Paul's tactic is clear from the outset: describe the actual, ideal plan or mechanism of salvation, then use that as a foundation for drawing conclusions about specific matters that derive from that plan.

Apostle designates somebody who has actually seen the risen Lord, and who has taken that revelation as a call to ministry. It comes from the Greek, *apostello*, to send. *Gospel* (NIV) is the translation of the Greek *euangelion*, which means *good news*. The term has become hackneyed through over- and misuse, but it remains an important technical term. The Gospel is a very specific body of propositional truth about events in heaven and on Earth, both eternal and historic, that serves as a sufficient, if not comprehensive, revelation of how God deals with his creation. The idea that the Gospel contains a spiritual component should not suggest that there is a vagueness or a fluidity in God's actions, intentions, and expectations. God gives freely to his creatures, but he gives on a very specific basis. It is this basis that Paul refers to when he talks about the Gospel.

VV. 2–3

At the heart of this Gospel is the notion that there are two actors involved in a moral drama. There is God, the Creator, and man, the creature—two actors, two moral agents, and as we shall see, two problems. The bridge between the two is the long-awaited Messiah, or Anointed One, the Christ, Jesus. Jesus used two terms for himself: Son of God and Son of Man. Being both fully divine and fully human, only he could make this claim. This apparent paradox of two natures in one man was used by Jesus himself to silence his detractors and also to explicate the tension it implies. On the one hand, Jesus the Son of God dwells in unapproachable light; he is the Wisdom of God and the judge of all mankind. As demonstrated by the Transfiguration, when we see him as he really is, we are blinded and terrified. On the other hand, as Son of Man, Jesus is our brother and friend, who is readily approached and apprehended by the most humble child. Paul is getting his audience ready for the fact that God, who is God of *all* humanity, has nevertheless chosen a Jew in a specific time and place in history to enact his redemptive plan. A Jewish Messiah, yes, but as Son of Man, also a Savior and Lord for all, including Gentiles.

V. 4

Verse 4 is the conclusion of the first chiasmus: Jesus Christ is God's Anointed One, as validated by his resurrection from the dead. The resurrection must be appreciated on at least two levels. On the one hand, it means that

Jesus is no longer in the grave, but is alive and reigns as Lord. He's not here; he's in heaven. On another level, it's a historical fact with profound forensic significance. The resurrection is proof that Good Friday worked. That is, by going to the cross and dying for a lost and sinful humanity, Sin has been dismantled and sins atoned for. The cross completes once and for all the sacrifice that Jewish ritual could only hint at, removing the moral divide that separated God from Man. As of Genesis chapter 3, God is at enmity with Man, and Man is at enmity with God. There are now two problems resulting from the Fall: there is moral guilt on our part, then there is powerlessness to reform our nature or restore our position. The resurrection is Jesus returning to life, and in doing so, conquering death. Death was the penalty for Sin, and once Sin was destroyed, the penalty, death, was removed. Jesus' ongoing life is proof that we will never be confronted with our sins, for they no longer exist from God's point of view. Ideas that Christ's sacrifice for Sin is somehow limited or restricted are nonsense. There is no limit to the efficacy or power of the death of Christ. There are two judgments. The first was on Sin and took place on Good Friday. The Second, which has yet to take place for the living at least, is not on Sin, but on fruitlessness. As of Good Friday, all are *justified*, to use a term we shall encounter again. Not all, however, are *saved*, another term we shall come across later in this letter. Any limitation on salvation comes not from defects in the Cross, but from defects in our response to the resurrected Jesus Christ, who aspires to be not only our Savior, but also our Lord.

VV. 5–7

Grace. Perhaps the most misunderstood word in Paul's vocabulary. Grace does not refer to some vague benevolent disposition on the part of God towards believers. Like other terms Paul uses, this one is very, very specific, and its impact is lost if we don't define it properly. Grace means *Christ in us*. It is a person, Jesus, who lives in us as Spirit, Holy Spirit. Grace is understood to be God's willingness to cleanse us through the sacrificial death of Jesus, and then, as of Pentecost, to live in us and do through us what we can't do for ourselves. There are many terms for the possibility that Jesus might live in us: baptism in the Holy Spirit, regeneration, new birth, etc. There is a great deal of misunderstanding about these terms, but there should not be. Man has two problems as enumerated previously: guilt and powerlessness. Our guilt is dealt with when Jesus died for us on the Cross, and we were placed in Christ forensically, legally. This is Luther's passive righteousness. One problem down, one to go. Though justified by the death of Christ, we are still incapable of reform beyond having a knowledge that we have and will continue to fall short of moral perfection. God's solutions match the problems, and they both involve his son, Jesus. Jesus' death solves our moral dilemma, and his Life solves our behavioral problem. Suffice it to say that if forgiveness is the first half of the Gospel, then Grace, Christ in us, is the second.

Nations or *Gentiles* (NIV). No sooner does Paul get through the preliminaries than he tackles his main objective: to resolve once and for all the question of God's plan of reconciling all of humanity to himself, Jew and Gentile alike. The Gentiles are looked down upon by the Jewish Christians. The Jews are having a hard time setting aside their prejudice and actual hatred of Gentiles, who they feel are inferior to themselves in every conceivable way. Paul starts out by saying that not only are Gentiles called no less than Jews, but that they, too, are loved by God and destined to be saints.

Called. More on this concept anon, but suffice it to say that in Paul's mind, calling has to do with the activity of the Holy Spirit as experienced by an individual in their particular life, not a sovereign decision by God about a person's spiritual destiny.

Thanksgiving for the Romans' faithfulness, Paul's prayers and plans[2]

8 First, I give thanks to my God through Jesus Anointed for you all, because your **faithfulness** is **proclaimed** in all the world.

9 My witness is God,

whom I serve in my spirit in his son's good news,

that without ceasing I make mention of you 10 always in my prayers, asking that somehow now at last I may succeed by God's will in coming to you.

11 For I long to see you, that I may share with you some spiritual gift to strengthen you,

12 that is, to be encouraged together with you by each other's faithfulness, both yours and mine.

13 I do not want you to be unaware, brothers, **that often**

I have longed

to come to you—

and I have been unable

until now—

that I may have some fruit also among you, as well as among the other nations.

14 To both Greeks and foreigners, to both learned
and ignorant, I am obligated.
15 So I am eager to preach *the* good news also to you in
Rome.
16 For I am not ashamed of the good news,
for God's Power is for salvation to everyone who is faithful—
Jew first, also Greek,
17 for in it *(in the good news)* God's justfulness is **revealed** by **faithfulness**
to **faithfulness**, as it is written: "The just *one* by faithfulness[3] will live."[4]

[2] 1:8–17 The second of five divisions of this letter. Parallel with 15:14—16:23. Compare 1:13 with 15:22–23.

[3] 1:17 *Faithfulness.* The Hebrew word in Habakkuk 2:4, translated here as "faithfulness," means "firmness, steadfastness, faithfulness, trust, fidelity." It appears in the Hebrew Bible 49 times. Only once, in Habakkuk 2:4, is it translated "faith" by the KJV. The KJV translates it: faithfulness 18 times, truth 13, faithfully 5, office 5, faithful 3, faith 1 (here), stability 1, steady 1, truly 1, verily 1. The LXX (which Paul quotes) translated it here with a Greek word, which Bauer-Danker-Arndt-Gingrich's Greek-English Lexicon (Third Edition, 2000) defines as: 1. faithfulness, reliability, fidelity, commitment, assurance, oath, troth, proof, pledge; 2. trust, confidence, faith; 3. body of faith/belief/teaching. At least when it applies to God, as in 3:3, it is usually translated "faithfulness."

[4] 1:17 Parallel with 1:8. This is restated in 3:21–26; 4:12,16; Phlp 3:9–11, and restates Gal 2:16; 3:11.

VV. 8–15

These verses start a second minor chiasmus. Paul wants to visit, and he may be understood as both seeking an invitation and warning them that when he does come, there will be an expectation that they understand the Gospel and are dealing with this Jew/Gentile distinction in a creative way. Note how he says, "other nations" or "other Gentiles" (NIV), confirming the fact that the Roman church was largely Gentile in composition. He even refers to Jews as "foreigners" or "non-Greeks" (NIV), to turn the tables completely on Jews who feel they have the upper moral hand in this dispute. He even uses parallelism to imply Jews may be *ignorant* or *foolish* (NIV).

V. 16

Salvation. Again, this is a technical term with a very specific meaning for Paul. To him, it is not interchangeable with justification, which is a very different matter. Justification doesn't concern him as much as salvation, because the former is a *fait accompli*. Salvation, by contrast, does not involve just God's sovereign action, but also man's cooperation. As we shall see later, God justified all humanity without our knowledge, permission, understanding, or consent. He just did it on his own, as the account of Abraham in Genesis 15 makes clear. The smoking firepot and flaming torch, variously the father and the son, pass between the sacrificed animals while Abraham sleeps; he plays no role whatsoever. This is why we baptize babies, because their lack of appreciation and participation is the perfect model of how we, even the cognizant adult, cannot add to or affect the sacrifice of Christ on the cross. At the last supper, Jesus says the bread and wine represent his body and blood in a *new* covenant, the *old* obviously being what Abraham viewed. Just as our bodies require food and drink to live, our spirits need the indwelling Spirit of Jesus, Grace, to live. This is salvation: *Christ in us*. This is by no means universal or a done deal. Salvation is therefore Paul's main concern, because though all are justified, not all are saved.

Is faithful or *believes* (NIV). The former translation is preferred. Greeks think belief refers to intellectual assent. To the Jew, this is absurd. Whereas Greek thought is analytic, taking things apart to focus on how the constituent parts work, the Jew finds this all irrelevant. The Jew, to his credit, is concerned with weightier matters: agency, purpose, and result, not process.[1] Belief to a Jew has nothing to do with the mind, but with the heart. This is why Jesus spoke in parables. The parable format requires that the hearer exercise their will in finding the meaning. Jesus never threw his pearls before swine, and he spoke in enigmatic terms and forms that were designed to confound the casual listener who had no intention of conforming their will to the message they were given. For a Jew, belief meant moral obedience as opposed to mental revelation. How can you know something and not let it reform you? As James points out, the demons believe in the Greek sense and shudder;[2] the knowledge produces no essential moral change. There is a great deal of

1. Another way to say the same thing would be to make a distinction between science, the fruit of the Western mind, and philosophy, the Eastern root. I quote Will Durant: "Shall we be more technical? Science is analytical description, philosophy is synthetic interpretation. Science wishes to resolve the whole into parts, the organism into organs, the obscure into the known. It does not inquire into the values and ideal possibilities of things, nor into their total and final significance; it is content to show their present actuality and operation, it narrows its gaze resolutely to the nature and process of things as they are. . . . But the philosopher is not content to describe the fact: he wishes to ascertain its relation to experience in general, and thereby to get at its meaning and its worth; he combines things in interpretive synthesis; he tries to put together, better than before, that great universe-watch which the inquisitive scientist has analytically taken apart. . . . Science gives us knowledge, but only philosophy can give us wisdom." Durant, *The Story of Philosophy*, xxvii.

2. Jas 2:19.

debate amongst Christian thinkers regarding this matter of belief and the effect it has on our eternal status. Martin Luther spoke of being justified *when* one believed.[3] The sinner's prayer is often formulated in a way that suggests that we are saved when we believe, when we say the magic words. There will be more discussion on this important point in coming pages, but strictly speaking, nothing changes in our spiritual standing because of intellectual revelation. God cares more for behavior than doctrine, and being faithful implies moral compliance as opposed to mere intellectual assent.[4]

V. 17

The mother lode of soteriology. This is the verse that converted Martin Luther. The key word is *God's*, as in God's possession, or *from* (NIV). That is, righteousness is not a descriptor of a man who does right things; but rather, it is an ascription, a status conferred upon the pious man by God himself. In other words, Christ's righteousness is ascribed to us, independently of our being actually righteous. The righteousness is "from God," not from us. It was won by Christ but awarded to us. *Faith*, like belief, is a word that means different things to different people, and especially people with differing hermeneutics. To the Jew, faith means not just believing some proposition in an intellectual sense, but rather an active acceptance of a truth and a willingness to operate in the light of that truth. It's not, as Oswald Chambers says, a tenacious holding on for fear of falling off, but rather a robust conviction that this alternate reality holds promise for us.[5]

Jews and Gentiles are equal before God[5]
Jews and Gentiles have both dishonored God[6]
Gentiles are without excuse[7]

18 Revealed is
    the vengeance
        of God
            from heaven
            against all godlessness and injustice
        of people
    who the truth in injustice
suppress.

3. Luther, *Commentary*, 66.
4. Matt 21:31.
5. Chambers, *My Utmost,* February 22.

19 For what can be known about God is plain to them, because God to them has made *it* plain.

20 His invisible *attributes*,

from creation of *the* world, by the *things* created are understood *and* clearly seen,

both his eternal power and deity.

So they are without excuse.

21 For, knowing God, not as God did they glorify or thank *him*.

Instead, they became futile in their thinking,

and darkened was their uncomprehending heart.

22 Claiming to be wise, they became fools,

23 and exchanged the glory of the immortal God for a likeness of an image of mortal man and birds and four-footed animals and reptiles.

24 Therefore, **God handed them over**

in the lusts of their hearts to impurity so as to disgrace their bodies among themselves,

25 those who exchanged God's truth for a lie

and worshiped and served the creature rather than the Creator,

who is blessed into the ages! Amen.

26 Because of this **God handed them over** to passions of disgrace.

Their females exchanged natural intercourse for unnatural;

27 likewise also the males,

leaving the natural intercourse with the female,

burned with their lust for one another,

males with males committing the shameless;

and receiving in themselves the due return for their deviation.

[5] 1:18—15:13 ABCCBA. The central of five divisions. A's: Jews and Gentiles have both dishonored God; Jews and Gentiles, glorify God together, as brothers. B's: Jews and Gentiles equal under faithfulness; be members of one another, as one body in Anointed, under God's will. C's: in Anointed all are reconciled to God; Israel and Gentiles are interdependent for salvation.

[6] 1:18—3:20 ABBA. Parallel with 14:1—15:13.

[7] 1:18–32 ABBA: Parallel with 3:1–20. A's: what and why. B's: how. A classic summary of Gentiles, as in Wisdom 13–14: estranged from God, unholy, unclean, abnormal, alien, idolaters (verse 23), that is, Gentiles. This is not how a Jew, like Paul, would describe Jews. Paul's description of Jews is in 2:17—3:20 and chapters 9–11.

V. 18

Wrath (NIV) or *vengeance* This is a very, very important concept that has a specific meaning when used by Paul. This term was used by John the Baptist, Jesus, and the apostle John, but never as much as by Paul. It refers not to some emotion on God's part, but rather a judgment on humanity based on God's intolerance for those who ignore his plan of redemption. This wrath takes the form of judgment both now, in this life and in this world, and also the final judgment depicted in Matthew 25 and Revelation 20. These two passages are parallel accounts of when all will be judged according to the extent to which we cooperated with God's redemptive plan or attempted to thwart it. The current evidence of God's wrath is the hardening of man's heart towards his only means of salvation, which is the life of Christ in us. Jacobus Arminius was careful to point out that God does not harden hearts, also called deluding thinking, on an arbitrary basis.[6] He hardens those who engage in wrong worship. Note the order of the words: *godlessness and injustice* or *wickedness* (NIV). Wrong worship, godlessness, leads inevitably to wrong behavior, wickedness. In the Garden we were three-part people: spirit, mind, and body. With the Fall our spirit was so attenuated that we became incapable of living spiritual lives. The body, which speaks loudly, invariably comes to dominate the mind, and we become irrational creatures. We act according to our impulses and temptations, then we rationalize the behavior *ex post facto* with our minds. God's intention—that our spirit inform our thinking and our thinking control our bodies—is completely reversed when our spirit remains unregenerate.

Suppress the truth (NIV). Unregenerate people hate cognitive dissonance and are very interested in justifying their behavior. By and large, they do not tolerate those who in word or deed attest to the existence and preeminence of a spiritual dimension. Blame shifting, "The woman you gave me gave me to eat and I ate," is the first sign of Sin.[7] There is always a body of rationalization that goes along with Sin, and it centers around a denial of God's existence and his involvement in the created order. Incredible amounts of energy are expended in an attempt to discredit the first principles of theism. Scientism or naturalism are hallowed as not only explaining the process of natural systems, but also the purpose. Yet here Paul argues that the created order is evidence in and of itself of God's existence and benevolence. Even the most jaded atheists can't explain how the world as we know it has come about given the limited time available and the second

6. Arminius, "Analysis," 502.

7. Gen 3:12.

law of thermodynamics. Entropy always triumphs over order, unless there is outside intervention. Yet to admit that the wonder and perfection of the created order is somehow a gift designed to bless us and turn our thoughts to our Creator is to indict atheistic epistemology. God can't exist, because if he did, atheists would have to change their thinking and ultimately their behavior. Their system, where wants define needs and actions are value-free, would all fall apart. If nothing else, atheists are consistent, and they know that if the cosmos around them is created and not an accident, then their world is of necessity turned upside down.

VV. 19–20

By the things created are clearly understood. The beauty, order, and consistency of creation is designed to point beyond itself to the beauty, order, and consistency of the Creator. The temptation from time immemorial is to worship creation for its own sake and not perceive that it is in fact a manifestation of the attributes of its author. In Paul's time, people readily ascribed ultimate importance to creation, while missing out on the spiritual message it was established to communicate. Nothing has changed to our present day.

VV. 21–23

Knowing God or *they knew God* (NIV). The conscience is not fallen, in spite of what John Calvin says.[8] Paul points out later on in chapter 7 that we can know right, it's just that we cannot do it. Here Paul defines worship as glorifying God and giving thanks to him. Wrong worship has consequences. Note the progression from verse 21a to 21b. Worship is determinative, and *thinking* is consequential. When we worship amiss, God imparts a delusion in our thinking and a hardness to our hearts. Thus, he imposes a solitude, spiritual isolation, on the atheist in keeping with their implicit request. Through wrong worship they have asserted their independence and asked that God depart from their midst. In deference to our free will, God honors that request, but in leaving he takes with him that "infinite abyss" to which Pascal alludes, and the person is the poorer for it.[9] Appetite for God is a gift,

8. Calvin, *Institutes*, 251–252.

9. "What else does this craving, and this helplessness, proclaim but that there was once in man a true happiness, of which all that now remains is the empty print and trace? This he tries in vain to fill with everything around him, seeking in things that are not there the help he cannot find in those that are, though none can help, since this infinite abyss can be filled only with an infinite and immutable object; in other words,

and when we lose it, even the ability to receive new revelation is attenuated, as per the author of the Letter to the Hebrews.[10] Elsewhere Paul speaks of our conscience being seared as with a hot iron, and this is what he's referring to here.[11] Man is naturally drawn to worship. If he denies God his place, then his worship takes on degraded form and dimension. Perhaps he worships alcohol, a psychotropic plant, the desires of his body, or even the flora and fauna of the created order, including the climate. Worship continues because it is in our nature. It's just the object of worship that is degraded, and the worshipper takes on the characteristics of that to which he bows down.[12] The conclusion to the chiasmus consisting of verses 21–23 is verse 21c, where our heart, the seat of our spiritual sensitivity, is of necessity damaged through bad worship decisions. We do this to ourselves.

VV. 24–27

What follows in verses 24–27 are two chiasmata, as correctly delineated by Bailey, describing in detail the consequences of wrong worship and addled thinking. What Paul says, to the dismay of many, is that wrong thinking soon becomes wrong behavior, often wrong sexual behavior. It is not the goal of this commentary to deliver a comprehensive treatment of sexual and gender issues, which have proven to be profoundly divisive, breaking asunder most of the mainline Protestant denominations. Rather, it is my goal to properly read and expound on what Paul is saying here, that he might once again be allowed to contribute to the discussion.

The current debate about sex and gender issues centers around this one question: how are sexual ideation and gender identity established? Are they volitional, which is what the church has historically maintained, or are they products of our biological constitution and beyond our control? The modern perspective, that we are born one way or the other, has received formal recognition as the psychiatric profession no longer lists homosexuality as a deviance or illness and now considers it an alternative orientation. Freud himself felt homosexuality was the result of abnormal emotional development, though he did not attach moral significance to it.[13] This preference for a biological explanation of sexual orientation has put the church in a difficult position. If sexual preference is not volitional but received,

by God himself." Pascal, *Pensées*, 75.

10. Heb 6:5–6.

11. 1 Tim 4:2.

12. Ps 115:8.

13. Freud, "Historical Notes," 786–787.

Christians appear to be demanding change that is not only impossible, but immoral. As Jeremiah says, "Can the Ethiopian change his skin or the leopard its spots?"[14] And what of the broader, more compelling commands that we are to love and accept one another without discriminating?

Verses 24a and 26a seem, at first glance, to give credence to the modern view that homosexuals and those experiencing gender dysphoria are in fact merely being honest about thoughts and feelings not of their own making. God has "handed them over," and as Paul says later in this letter, "Then why does God still blame us? For who can resist his will?"[15] An honest treatment of the text, however, requires that we read verses 24–27 in the larger context of the verses that precede them. Indeed, Bailey points out that verses 18–32 constitute a chiasmus in the form of ABBA, with the A sections addressing *what* and *why*, and the B's *how*. Thus, verses 24 and 25 are a B chiasmus, as are verses 26 and 27. They appear to be parallel accounts and therefore repetitive, but upon examination they also differ. I'll deal with them one at a time.

Verse 24a corresponds with verse 25c, and it deals with God's sovereign action of "handing over" to which humans are subject without recourse. Again, this is support for the modern view of divine determinism in sexual matters. Verses 24b and 25b, however, point out that God's monergistic action is not independent of human decision, but is itself based on the worship practices of people, something over which they *do* have control. The conclusion, verse 25a, states why God has made worship determinative, and that is because worship must be based upon ultimate spiritual reality and truth.

Similarly, verses 26 and 27 constitute a chiasmus that starts out essentially repeating verse 24a about handing people over. But then instead of dwelling on the importance of worship as a causal factor, it goes in the opposite direction and describes the behavior that wrong worship and wrong thinking produce. Paul indicts both female and male homosexuality, using adjectives that leave no doubt as to his disapproval. Readers may wonder why Paul focuses on sexual behavior, and this has led many to conclude that he was an unmarried prude who simply didn't like sex.[16] It is more fruitful to recognize the causal sequence of his argument, though, that worship controls thought, and thought controls behavior. In other words, the spiritual domain informs the intellectual, and the intellectual informs the physical. This is an important scenario, because the church has often erred by

14. Jer 13:23.

15. Rom 9:19.

16. 1 Cor 6:18–20.

focusing on behavioral reform without realizing that behavior is merely the tail on the dog. To engage in effective ministry, the church must place less emphasis on what converts are doing or even thinking, and more on how converts are worshiping. Attempts to lift Paul's proscriptions out of their proper rhetorical context is to misrepresent him and miss this important distinction between cause and consequence. The conclusion of this second chiasmus, verse 27b, states the ideal of gender roles and sexual activity. Sex is supposed to be the means by which humans obey the first commandment encountered in the Bible, that they should be fruitful and multiply.[17] Note that this commandment was given before the Fall, and thus represents God's unwavering desire that his creation should be full and not empty.[18] If sexual reproduction is in fact central to God's plan of creation, we have new insight into why God might be displeased with not only homosexual activity, which cannot produce fruit, but also in our own day with abortion, which similarly divorces the sex act from the possibility of childbearing.

Receiving in themselves the due return for their deviation. If it is true that any separation of sexual activity from God's mandate for producing children is contrary to God's express will, we can then understand why homosexuality can grieve the Holy Spirit and engender spiritual loss. The created order, rightly understood, reflects the spiritual order that superintends over it. When God leaves, he takes his mercy with him, partly as punishment but also to testify to the danger of living without God's grace, here and in the life to come.

28 And because they did not think *it* worthy
to acknowledge
God,
God
handed them over
to a worthless mind to do what is not worthy—
29 becoming filled with every injustice, evil, greed, malice—
full of envy, murder, rivalry, deceit, sprite—
gossips, 30 slanderers, God-haters—
tyrants, arrogant *ones*, boasters, schemers of evils, disobedient to parents—
31 senseless, faithless, heartless, ruthless—
32 those who, acknowledging God's sentence
that those doing such things

17. Gen 1:28.

18. Isa 45:18.

are worthy of death,
not only do them
but even approve of doing *them*.

VV. 28–32

Paul reiterates his argument about the sequence of how worship determines thought and thought determines behavior. This is why it's impossible to try to change people's behavior long-term without changing their worship. For too long, the church has said to transgressors, "Your behavior is evil and outside the bounds of decency. Stop what you're doing, *then* come to church." The average person, when confronted with the dictates of Scripture, usually tries to comply. When they fail, as they must if motivated only by their own resolve, they have two choices. Either they can try harder and become religious hypocrites, or they can give up trying, reject scriptural testimony, and become their own moral standard. In neither case do they do what God intends. What God intends is that we reform our worship first, then our thinking can become unclouded, and only then our behavior can be redressed. What the church should be saying is something along these lines, "Come as you are to worship, be prepared to be changed."

Those who reject God start to think amiss and to behave in keeping with their darkened minds. The wrath of God is not limited to some future time and distant world. It starts now. When we go within the radius of the chain with which the Devil is held, there are consequences even now.[19] This is both to bring the sinner to his senses and to serve as a warning to others who are watching.

There is a fraternity to evil. Transgressors want company. Mutual encouragement helps silence the conscience and fosters rationalization. Pilate and Herod were enemies until they collaborated in the execution of Jesus.[20]

19. Rev 20:1.

20. Luke 23:12

Chapter 2

PRÉCIS

In this chapter, Paul continues his diatribe about how both Jews and Gentiles have dishonored God. He started his argument by highlighting the gross immorality of the Gentile world, stating that even without the benefit of specific revelation as enjoyed by the Jews, Gentiles should know better. Now he turns away from the Gentiles specifically and makes a general case that no matter what our spiritual or cultural background, our behavior invites divine judgment. He goes on to refine his argument and address the sanctimonious Jew by name. Here he assaults the treasured possession of the Jew, circumcision, as a symbol of all that is wrong with seeking righteousness by observing the Law.

All who judge are self-condemned[8]

2 Therefore without excuse are you, O human, whoever judges.
For in what you judge another, yourself you condemn,
since the same *things* do you, who judges.

2 We know that God's judgment is according to truth against those who do such things.

3 Do you think this, O human,
who judges those doing such things
and does *the* same *things*,
that you will escape God's judgment?
4 Or, for the riches of his kindness and forbearance and patience,
do you have little regard,
not understanding

that God's kindness leads you to repentance?

[8] 2:1–16 ABA. Parallel with 2:17–29. A's: all who sin are without excuse. B: God's judgment is just.

VV. 1–3

Oh human or *you* (NIV). Paul immediately adopts an adversarial tone in addressing his audience and embarks on a diatribe. He just let the Gentiles have it in Chapter 1, where he rehearses how wrong worship leads to depraved thinking and terrible behavior. Now he sets out to show that Jews, who often adopt a sanctimonious and superior attitude towards Gentiles, are guilty in their own way. He doesn't say "You Jews . . . ." but he might as well have. Like a good marriage counselor, he spreads his harsh observations evenly between the two factions whose reconciliation he wants to engineer. His audience is for the most part Gentile, and by highlighting the shortcomings of the Jews, he is hoping to do two things. First, he wants to engage Gentiles who will feel they are finally understood, and second, he's making it clear that much of the fault for the conflicts within the church really can be laid at the feet of the Jews. He's had it with this controversy, and he's going to get to the root of it and deal it a death blow.

It's one thing to do wrong, and still another, in God's eyes, to do wrong while criticizing others who do it. Hypocrisy appears to be especially onerous to God. God is willing to forgive sins, but he demands that we also forgive the sins of others. The standard we use for others will be the same standard used for us.[1]

V. 4

In the parable of the good and bad seed, Jesus reveals that God tolerates sin in order to allow time for all who would repent and bear fruit to do so.[2] His concern is not so much to foil sinners as to bless the righteous. This is a consistent theme in the Scriptures; God is more pleased with obedience than he's distressed by sin. Note how David, described as a man after God's own heart, was nevertheless guilty of profound sin and error, including murder, adultery, and hubris.[3] We, too, should be more concerned about doing right

1. Matt 7:1–12.
2. Matt 13:24–30.
3. See Acts 13:22.

than avoiding wrong. The two are related, but positive obedience outweighs disobedience every time.

> 5 By your hardness and unrepentant heart you are storing up for yourself vengeance on *the* day of vengeance and revelation of God's just judgment,
> 6 who "will give back to each according to his works"—
> 7 to those who by perseverance in doing good seek glory and honor and immortality:
> eternal life;
> 8 but to those who from self-seeking both disobey the truth and obey injustice:
> vengeance and fury;
> 9 trouble and distress
> upon every human soul that does evil, Jew first, also Greek,
> 10 but glory and honor and peace
> to everyone who does good, Jew first, also Greek.
> 11 "There is no favoritism with God."

VV. 5–11

A chiasmus focused on *vengeance* or *wrath* (NIV). Paul quotes Psalm 62:12, stating that there will be a reckoning based upon actions taken in this life. Paul goes on to explain just what this reckoning will be, for it is more than a crude retaliation for sins. Here is one of the great dilemmas of Christian moral thought: are we condemned for doing wrong, for sinning, or are we rewarded for doing right? Technically speaking, we are never judged for our sins as such. See Matthew 25, where the sheep and goats are separated according to how they treated Jesus in the person of others, specifically Christians. They are saved or condemned not on the basis of wrong they did, but on the basis of good they did or did not do.[4] Given the chance to serve Christ by serving those "brothers of mine," some did, and some did not. The evil here is the absence of good. Likewise in Revelation 20, all humanity is assembled and judged "according to what they had done." Here the criterion again is a positive one, their name had to be recorded in the book of life. Put another way, was the life of Jesus in them that they were truly alive? Alive in spirit as well as body? Jesus and Paul offer laundry lists of behaviors that are sinful and get us into spiritual trouble, as does John in his Revelation.

4. Jas 4:17.

Jesus even says to obdurate individuals, " . . . you will die in your sin."[5] We should not interpret this as meaning that we will be judged and condemned because of our sins, but that our lives apart from God will be characterized by sinful behavior. Sin does not cause condemnation, because all sins will be atoned for by the Cross. Sins accompany spiritual rebellion, however, and interfere with Christ's ability to operate as our Lord. Christ is the Savior of all, because that status was accorded to us by his obedience in going to the Cross. Justification is universal. Christ is not the Lord of all, however, because that status is particular to the individual. His Lordship can be accepted or refused, and that reveals the heart of each person. Verse 7 should not be viewed as an endorsement of Pelagianism, but rather as a description of the life that has been receptive to the working of the Holy Spirit. The sin of verse 8, similarly, is not the following of evil so much as the antecedent self-seeking and rejection of the truth. Again, wrong worship leads to wrong behavior. The latter is important only to the extent that it reveals the former.

Verse 9 is the conclusion of this chiasmus. Again, Paul's major objective is not to show how or why we're judged, but to show that Jew and Gentile alike are subject to judgment by God, according to the same standard. God does not show favoritism, even though people, Jews especially, would like to think he does.

> 12 All who have sinned without law will also perish without law, and all who have sinned under law will be judged by law.
>
> > 13 For not the hearers of law *are* just before God; rather, the doers of law will be justified.[9]
> >
> > > 14 For when Gentiles, those not having law, by nature do the law's requirements,
> > >
> > > > they, not having law, are a law to themselves.
> > >
> > > 15 They show the law's work written on their hearts,
> >
> > their conscience bearing witness and *their* thoughts on one side or another accusing or even defending *them*,
>
> 16 on *the* day when God judges the secrets of human hearts, according to my good news, by Anointed Jesus.

[9] 2:13 *Justified.* A legal technical term meaning "acquitted" or "found innocent of the charge." Used in Gal 2:16—5:4 and Rom 2:13—8:33. Paul appears to use it to refer to members of God's family, as in Gal 3:23–29 and Rom 3:27—4:2.

5. John 8:21.

VV. 12–16

Paul again appears to be proposing a retributive justice where sin is punished by death, whether one is Jewish or Gentile. And once again, his point is not to explicate exactly how we are judged, but rather to emphasize the fact that Jew and Gentile face the same dilemma. We are called to obey, but we cannot. Faced with this impossibility, we have to seek divine help. Help comes not through the Law, for the law demands results but does not confer aid. What helps is the presence of the Holy Spirit in our hearts, a reality who bears fruit whether one is Jewish or not. Indeed, the ministry of the Holy Spirit allows even Gentiles to obey God's moral dictates *by nature*, as per the conclusion in verses 14 and 15a. What was missing in their spiritual DNA, having been born outside the first covenant, will now be *written on their hearts*. Thus, a Gentile filled with the Spirit is able to please God whereas a Jew without the Spirit is not. His point is to undermine Jewish pride that they are still somehow superior to non-Jews, for since the coming of the Holy Spirit there is no advantage to being Jewish. The Spirit came to Jews first, to be sure, but it was not long before He came to Gentiles as well.[6]

A Jew who teaches the law and breaks it is self-condemned[10]

[Paul] 17 But you, if a Jew you call yourself
and you rely on *the* law
and you boast in God
18 and you know *his* will
and you discern what is best, being instructed from the law,

19 and you are confident that you are a guide of *the* blind,
a light of those in darkness,
20 a corrector of *the* foolish,
a teacher of children,
having the embodiment of knowledge and truth in the law—
21 One then, who teaches another, do you not teach yourself?
One who preaches not to steal, do you steal?
22 One who says not to commit adultery, do you commit adultery?
One who abhors idols, do you rob temples?

6. Acts 10.

23 You who boasts in *the* law,
by breaking the law you dishonor God.
24 For, "God's name because of you is blasphemed among the Gentiles,"
as it is written.

25 Circumcision indeed has value if you obey *the* law,
but if you are a lawbreaker your circumcision has become uncircumcision.
26 Therefore, if the uncircumcision keeps the law's requirements,
will not his uncircumcision be regarded as circumcision?
27 And the uncircumcision by nature that fulfills the law will condemn you
who, with *the* letter *of the law* and circumcision, *is* a lawbreaker

28 One is not a Jew outwardly,
nor *is* circumcision outward in flesh.
29 Rather, one *is* a Jew inwardly,
and circumcision *is* of heart, in spirit, not letter,
whose praise[11] *is* not from people but from God.

[10] 2:17–29 ABCBA. A's: the meaning of being a Jew, B's: the value of the law and the bodily mark of the law, C: boasting in the law and breaking it dishonors God.
[11] 2:29 *Praise* is the meaning of *Judah*, for which *Jew* is an abbreviation.

VV. 17–29

Note Bailey's footnote 10 on the chiasmus that this passage presents. Paul goes to the bottom of Jewish pride and mentions each of the ways in which they have historically considered themselves superior to Gentiles. Yes, they have the revelation, and yes, to the extent that the Law is understood, they have an advantage. But what is, in fact, the purpose of the Law? Clearly, God never intended the Law to be obeyed. These are crimes committed by everybody, Jew and Gentile alike. The Law cannot be obeyed in its entirety, because it goes beyond the ability of man to understand it, let alone conform to it. The Law involves intent as well as action, desire as well as deed, and as such, it is beyond any human capacity for obedience. Clearly, the purpose of the Law is twofold: to reveal God's moral perfection and to make us despair of ever being able to fulfill its demands. It is designed to make us realize our plight, to hunger for a Savior, and to usher our surrender. The Jews, particularly the Jewish religious authorities, however, did not get this. They thought it could be obeyed and that they were proof that it could. Paul gets down to the facts and points out that such thinking is absurd. Not only do the Jews fail, but their public failure gives Gentiles an excuse to dismiss the God the Jews claim to know.

Circumcision is profound in conception, yet superficial in execution. It was introduced for at least two purposes: one relating to human relations, one relating to divine. On the one hand, it was to remind the Jew that he was different from other people. Here was a visible sign—a sacrament, if you will—that in difference there is separation, in separation there is a calling, and in the calling there is hope of salvation. On the other hand, circumcision is to remind the Jew that he is dependent upon God. There is profound symbolism in the act itself, of cutting something off. We do not have a positive role in our salvation as Pelagius would have us believe. We have a role, to be sure, but it's negative. As such, circumcision is a metaphor for repentance.[7] It's the removal of something, rather than an addition; specifically, we are to remove our right to ourselves as asserted by Adam. When we remove the foreskin, we are saying that as the penis is the seat of our physical desire, so we must yield that and all our desires to God if we are to be accounted Holy. Put metaphorically, when the Jews were to cross the Jordan and enter the Holy Land, they had to be circumcised before doing so. The image is clear: the promised land is salvation, the foreskin is our will or identity, and the removal of the foreskin is the ceding of the will to God. God has a permanent claim on us, and we are to bear in our flesh a permanent acknowledgment of that claim.

Paul uses circumcision as a symbol of both national and religious identity—that which makes the Jew different. He goes on to point out, however, that it's just a symbol, not the inner reality that God's actually looking for. It's fully possible to look like a Jew but not act like one, just as it is also possible to be a Gentile yet act like a Jew. This is in full agreement with the encounter between Jesus and the woman from Syrian Phoenicia whose daughter was demon possessed. Jesus initially refused to help, for this woman didn't have the pedigree of a Jew that spoke of a genuine faith in God. When she protested and acknowledged the validity of Jewish primacy, Jesus relented. She proved herself to be Jewish in spirit, if not in body.[8]

7. Exod 12:48. Circumcision is to *precede* eating the Passover meal. John the Baptist is to *precede* Jesus and repentance is to *precede* realization of all Christ does for us.

8. Mark 7:24–30

Chapter 3

PRÉCIS

This chapter is an excellent example of how Paul uses tools of Hebrew rhetoric to make his point while keeping his audience engaged. He has just assaulted the bastion of Jewish pride, but now moderates his attack by honoring the history of specific revelation. As wonderful as Jewish history is, it is still not sufficient to meet the needs of a fallen humanity. The only thing that is sufficient is the life and death of Jesus of Nazareth, himself a Jew, but Savior and Lord of Gentiles as well. Paul reveals the only true source of righteousness.

Both Jews and Greeks are indicted under law[12]

[Jewish Teacher] 3 What then *is* the **advantage** of the Jew? Or what *is* the value of circumcision?

[Paul] 2 Much in every way! First, that they were entrusted with **God's very words.**[13] 3 What if some were unfaithful?[14] Will their unfaithfulness God's faithfulness[15] nullify?

[Jewish Teacher] 4 Not at all! God must be true, though "every human a liar," as it is written: "That you may be justified in your words, and win when you are accused."

[Paul] 5 But if our unjustfulness confirms God's justfulness, what are we to say? *That* God *is* unjust to take vengeance *on us Jews*? (I speak in a human way.)

[Jewish Teacher] 6 Not at all! For then how will God judge the world?

[Paul] 7 But if **God's truthfulness** excels by my falsehood to his glory, why am I still condemned as a sinner? 8 And *why* not, as we

are accused and as some affirm that we say, "Let us do evil that good
may come?"[16] Their condemnation is deserved.

[**Jewish Teacher**] 9 What then? Are we *Jews* at a **disadvantage**?

[**Paul**] Not at all!

For we have already indicted **both Jews and Greeks**, that all are under
sin, 10 as it is written:

"There is no one just, **not one**,"
11 "there is no one who understands,
there is no one who seeks God.
12 All have turned away,
together they are worthless,
there is no one who does good, ***not* even one**."

13 "Their **throat** *is* an opened grave,
with their **tongues** they deceive."
"Vipers' venom *is* under their **lips**."
14 "Their **mouth** is full of cursing and bitterness."

15 "Their **feet** *are* swift to shed blood,
16 ruin and misery *are* in their **ways**,
17 and *the* **way** of peace they have not known."
18 "There is no fear of God before their **eyes**."

19 Now we know that whatever the law says,
to those under the law it speaks
in order that every mouth
may be silenced
and accountable may be
all the world to God,
20 "because by works of law no flesh will be justified in his sight,"
for through law *comes* knowledge of sin.

12 3:1–20 ABBBA. Parallel with 1:18–32. A's: all are under law. B's: quotations from the Psalms, Is, Prov, Eccl.

13 3:2 *God's very words*. Not only the promise that Abraham's seed would be blessed (4:13), but also the promise that God would bless the Gentiles through Abraham's seed (Rom 4; Gen 12:3; 18:18; 22:18).

14 3:3 *Unfaithful.* In communicating God's promises to the Gentiles (see 2:17–24; 9:30—10:3; 15:7–13).

15 3:3 *Faithfulness.* Toward his promises to Abraham. This question is addressed more fully in chapters 9–11.

16 3:8 This question is addressed more fully in chapter 6.

VV. 1–20

Note Bailey's footnote about the symmetry in verses 1–20. The biblical quotes constitute the conclusion, in that Paul has scriptural authority to back up what he says in the A sections. He starts off by listing the real advantages Jews have by way of specific revelation. Before Abraham there was general revelation, best represented by the ministry of Melchizedek. Subsequently, God made himself known to individuals and groups on a haphazard basis, governed by a strict code of retributive justice. With Genesis 15, however, we are introduced to the idea that God will unilaterally undertake mankind's redemption, at cost to only himself. There will be something new and wonderful about how God will deal with Abraham's descendants as opposed to everybody else. First, they will be given the Scriptures, *the very words of God* (NIV). God is, after all, a God of the Word. In Genesis he speaks, and it comes to be. The interplay between the Jewish words for *spirit*, *breath*, and *speech* is well-documented.

God has chosen a specific people for two reasons. First, he wants to prove a point about human nature. He wants to show that no matter how much information we have, no matter how much hand-holding and encouragement, no matter how much privilege and advantage, people simply cannot attain moral success.[9] We fail, Pelagius, not because we don't know what's right, but because knowledge alone is inadequate. Being fallen people, our spirits are dead, and our bodies rage out of control. Our mind is a weak bedfellow to our bodies, rationalizing and justifying whatever whim seems most desirable. Second, God chose a people as a vehicle for setting things right. The Law would come through Moses to bring awareness of Sin; grace and truth would come through Jesus to satisfy the dictates of the Law and bring about its abolition. Jesus would be the promised descendant of Abraham who would bless the entire world.

Paul now deals with the problem of what, exactly, God is looking for by way of response from people. There are three distortions of God's plan of redemption Paul must deal with. He's already addressed two of them: the license of Gentiles who worship amiss and the legalism of Jews who

9. Exod 16:4b.

try to earn salvation through works. He now adds a third problem, that of Christians who say that if we're freely forgiven, behavior no longer matters: libertines or antinomians. Is salvation going to be universal, regardless of our response? Is it going to be arbitrary, based on God's whim without regard to the character of the individual, as John Calvin,[10] and even Martin Luther[11] in his German translation preface, contend? Is it going to be based on a system of moral merit, as Pelagius and the later Roman church would assert? Just how does this mechanism of salvation work? And how is it that God has instituted this program by choosing Israel, yet the plan is not exactly working? Paul wants to praise God for his perfection and wisdom, while at the same time pointing out that this preliminary covenant is full of flaws. The flaws are not in God's plan per se, but in man's response to that plan. In God's permissive will, there is room for error on man's part. Paul wants to point out who's to blame here, and it's not God.

The plan of redemption Paul is describing has two component parts. First there is the Law, which is designed to establish a moral standard for our behavior while mirroring God's own righteousness. Paul's critics have said that if God does indeed forgive, why not give him more opportunities for forgiving by deliberately doing evil?[12]

After a brief digression to silence his critics, Paul returns to his main argument, which is that Jew and Gentile alike are in spiritual trouble. Note that he doesn't say both sin, he says both are *under Sin*. *Sin* to Paul is more than wrong actions, more than an accumulation of human waywardness. It is a state of moral independence from God, triggered by Adam and Eve's rebellion, and in full operation to the present day amongst all people from birth. As of Good Friday, all humanity is justified, and our sins are no longer accounted to us. However, there is still a vestige of the Fall manifest in our character. We have a desire to act independently of God, to recommit

10. " . . . we say that God once established by his eternal and unchangeable plan those whom he long before determined once for all to receive into salvation, and those whom, on the other hand, he would devote to destruction." Calvin, *Institutes*, 931.

11. "In chapters 9, 10 and 11, St. Paul teaches us about the eternal providence of God. It is the original source which determines who would believe and who wouldn't, who can be set free from sin and who cannot. Such matters have been taken out of our hands and are put into God's hands so that we might become virtuous. It is absolutely necessary that it be so, for we are so weak and unsure of ourselves that, if it depended on us, no human being would be saved. The devil would overpower all of us. But God is steadfast; his providence will not fail, and no one can prevent its realization." Luther, *Preface*, lines 160–163.

12. Heinrich Heine is rumored to have been asked on his death bed if he expected God to forgive him. He apparently said, "Of course he will forgive me, that's his job." Quoted by Meissner, "Gott wird mir verzeihen, das ist sein Beruf." Meissner, *Heinrich Heine. Erinnerungen*, Chapter 5.

Adam's sin, and operate as if Adam were our Lord. Paul quotes a conflation of Psalms 14, 53, 5, 140, and 10, with Ecclesiastes 7 and Isaiah 59, to make his point. Being under sin is open, deliberate, and culpable rebellion against God that manifests itself in acts of wickedness toward both God and our fellow man.

Paul adds to our understanding of the purpose of the Law by pointing out, in verse 19, that one of its goals is to see that every mouth is stopped. Whenever we do right and seek to generate righteousness on our own, we are to take stock and realize that no amount of effort, desire, self-abnegation, or anything else will work. This is wonderful news to the sinner, who like Martin Luther, sought through self-effort to effectuate a righteousness of his own.[13] It's like hitting your head with a hammer; it feels great when you stop. No matter how hard we chase the goal, it doesn't matter because the goal we are chasing is the wrong one. God has instituted a plan of redemption for all mankind, and it's perfect. Because it's perfect, it doesn't have to be duplicated or mimicked. The only way it can fail is if a person tries to institute a different, and by definition ineffective, plan of their own devising. Paul now turns from denigrating our arrogant and futile efforts to justify ourselves—be it through obedience to the Law for Jews or license for Gentiles—and proffers the correct path.

Jews and Gentiles equal under faithfulness[17]
Jews and Gentiles equal under Jesus' faithfulness

[**Paul**] 21 But now apart from law
God's justfulness has been made known,
being witnessed to by the law and the prophets.
22 God's justfulness *has been made known*
through Jesus Anointed's faithfulness to all who are faithful.

There is no distinction.[18]
23 For all have sinned and fall short of God's glory,
24 being justified freely by his grace through the deliverance in Anointed Jesus,

13. Luther wrote to his mentor, Johann von Staupitz, vicar general for the Augustinian order in Germany, "For I hoped I might find peace of conscience with fasts, prayer, and the vigils with which I miserably afflicted my body, but the more I sweated it out like this, the less peace and tranquility I knew." Quoted by Kittelson, *Luther the Reformer*, 84.

25 whom God put forward as a means of conciliation through *Jesus'* faithfulness in *shedding* his blood,

for demonstration of his [God's] justfulness

because of the passing over of the sins of the past 26 in God's forbearance,

for demonstration of his justfulness at the present time,

that he is just and *the* justifier of the one *who is* from Jesus' faithfulness.

[17] 3:21—4:25 ABA. Parallel with 12:1—13:14.

[18] 3:22 *No distinction*, which makes Jews alone the recipients of God's mercy. Another answer to 3:9a.

VV. 21–26

God's or *from God* (NIV). Only God is righteous, and therefore righteousness can only come from him. In his plan of redemption, instead of demanding that humans produce righteousness through their own efforts, as the Law suggests, God will confer his own righteousness on people. It is as if we each have an account with God, and that account is filled with God's moral currency, not our own. And note who benefits from this accreditation: all of us. Just as all sin, all are justified freely by this sacrifice of atonement. Now there are several qualifiers in this discourse, specifically . . . *to all who believe . . . through faith in his blood . . . those who have faith in Jesus* (NIV). This led Luther, among others, to say that when we exhibit faith, the benefits of Christ's sacrifice are credited to our account and we are justified. I would argue that Paul is emphasizing our response to this gift from God in order to show that Jew and Gentile alike are to be held accountable to God for responding to this free gift. It is not as though we are justified only when we have faith, as that limits the power of the Cross and makes redemption dependent upon us, which is a Pelagian error. A better interpretation of Paul's general argument—and this will be made clearer in later chapters—is that justification is a *fait accompli* based on Christ's atoning sacrifice. This justification applies to sins committed even prior to that event. In this way, and only in this way, is God able to remain perfect and just himself and to offer justification to the sinful humanity he is endeavoring to reclaim. By listing these seeming qualifiers to what I consider to be an unqualified gift, Paul seeks to show that the appellations of Jew and Gentile fall away when the Law is replaced with a new opportunity: faith in Christ. Fiduciary justification does not depend on faith in Christ, as it has an objective status of its own. It is realized and beheld, however, when faith in Christ allows the eyes of our hearts to be opened to this preexisting and abiding legal reality. We are not justified when we believe, we realize we are already justified when we believe.[14]

Jews and Gentiles equal under one God who justifies both through faithfulness

[Jewish Teacher] 27 Where then *is* the *basis for* boasting?

[Paul] It has been excluded!

[Jewish Teacher] By what law? Of works?

[Paul] No, but by a law of faithfulness. 28 For we consider a person to be justified by faithfulness apart from works of law.

29 Or *is God* the God of Jews only?

Not also of Gentiles?

[Jewish Teacher] Yes, also of Gentiles.

[Paul] 30 If indeed God *is* one[19]

he will justify *the* circumcised by faithfulness and *the* uncircumcised through faithfulness.

[Jewish Teacher] 31 Are we then nullifying *the* law through faithfulness?[20]

[Paul] Not at all! Rather, we uphold *the* law.

[19] 3:30 *God* is one. The argument in verses 29–30 is based on the Shema (Deut 6:4).
[20] 3:31 This question is addressed more fully in 7:1—8:8.

VV. 27–31

Boasting. The Jews boasted. Paul says such boasting is groundless, to say nothing of rude. But once again he is aware that faith may have a superficial interpretation, and that Christians can say, as Oswald Chambers derisively

14. Oswald Chambers writes, "I am not saved by believing; I realize I am saved by believing. It is not repentance that saves me; repentance is the sign that I realize what God has done in Christ Jesus. The danger is to put the emphasis on the effect instead of on the cause—'It is my obedience that puts me right with God, my consecration.' Never! I am put right with God because prior to all, Christ died. When I turn to God and by belief accept what God reveals I can accept, instantly the stupendous Atonement of Jesus Christ rushes me into a right relationship with God, and by the supernatural miracle of God's grace I stand justified, not because I am sorry for my sin, not because I have repented, but because of what Jesus has done. The spirit of God brings it with a breaking, all-over light, and I know, though I do not know how, that I am saved." Chambers, *My Utmost*, October 28.

observes, "Christ died for me, I go scot free."[15] Although the Law as such is fulfilled and rendered nugatory by Christ's death of the Cross, nevertheless its moral requirements abide. The Law has been fulfilled, not by us, but by Jesus. All its moral aspects remain intact, and just because we are considered as having fulfilled its requirements through Christ's obedience, we cannot reject the importance of moral behavior while we yet live. As of Good Friday, sin becomes a secondary, not a primary, concern. Though Sin has lost its power to condemn, it has not lost its power to grieve the Holy Spirit. To the extent that we reassert Adam's right to decide what is right or wrong, as symbolized by eating the fruit of the Tree of the Knowledge of Good and Evil, Sin can still kill and devour. It is as if all of sins were reduced to One Sin, and that is to follow Adam as Lord instead of Jesus. In making this moral decision, we grieve the Holy Spirit, find ourselves powerless to obey Jesus and bear fruit for him, remain incapable of doing right, and fail to have our name written in the Book of Life. Understood this way, we see that Sin cannot interfere with having Jesus as Savior, but it can interfere with having him as Lord. To not have Jesus as Lord is to become subject to God's wrath reserved for those who may count on Jesus to justify themselves but who will not consent to obey him.[16]

15. Chambers, *My Utmost*, October 29.

16. Matt 7:21–23.

Chapter 4

PRÉCIS

One of the salient characteristics of Hebrew thought and history is repetition. God tends to do things twice. First he does them in a temporary, local, and limited way. Then he does the same thing in a manner that is permanent, universal, and spiritual. Paul now shows how circumcision is a limited adumbration of the unlimited gift of what Bailey translates as *justfulness*, or righteousness. A title that can be given for this section of the letter, extending from 3:21 to 4:25, a B section, is "Jews and Gentiles alike can receive righteousness from God."

> [**Jewish Teacher**] 4 What then shall we say that Abraham found, our forefather according to flesh?
> 2 For if Abraham was justified by works, he has reason for boasting.

VV. 1–2A

Bailey feels rightly these verses belong to the preceding chiasmus that started with verse 3:27. They are placed here simply because of the chapter divisions that were imposed on Paul's letter. Logically they correspond with verse 3:27, which states that faith precludes boasting based on the flesh.

> **Jews and Gentiles equal under Abraham's faithfulness**[21]
> [**Paul**] But not before God.
> 3 For what does the scripture say?
> "Abraham put faith in God and it was counted to him as justfulness."[22]
> 4 Now to one who works,

the pay is not counted as a gift
but as a debt.
5 But to one who does not work,
but puts faith in him who justifies the godless,
his faith is counted as justfulness.
6 So also David declares the blessedness of the person to whom God counts justfulness apart from works:
7 "Blessed *are they* whose transgressions are forgiven, and whose sins are covered.
8 Blessed *the* man whose sin *the* Lord will not take into account."

9 *Is* this blessing then upon the circumcised,
or also upon the uncircumcised?
We say, "Faith was counted to Abraham as justfulness."
10 How then was it counted?
In circumcision or in uncircumcision?
Not in circumcision but in uncircumcision.
11 And he received a sign of circumcision—a seal of the justfulness of the faith that *he had* in uncircumcision—
that he might be father of all who are faithful during uncircumcision so that justfulness might be counted to them,
12 and father of circumcision to those who are not only of circumcision but who also walk in the footsteps of the faithfulness in uncircumcision of our father Abraham.

[21] 4:2b–25 ABCDCBA. The A's: faith counted as justfulness. The B's: when the promise was given. The C's: the promise is by faith to all. D: the promise is by faithfulness so it may be a gift guaranteed to all.

[22] 4:3 Also quoted at 4:9,22–23 and discussed in Gal 3:6–29. In Gen 22:18 "obey" is used for "put faith."

VV. 2B–12

Note Bailey's footnote about the chiasmus extending from 4:2b–25. This places the conclusion as verse 16. In the ascending argument, Paul seeks to buttress his assertions about Jews being unable to obey the Law and earn righteousness on their own by citing the case of the first Jew, Abraham. He, too, had to *find* or *discover* (NIV) something new. God never works in the old ways, and whatever the subject, progress occurs when people are able to withstand a paradigm shift and start to think in new ways. The idea that we are judged according to our own merits and self-effort is endemic to Man; we are fundamentally arrogant and always seeking to earn our keep. For Abraham to witness the ratification of a covenant without his participation must have been a novel revelation.

It always works to introduce an innovation by showing that in fact, it's always been done that way: it's as if Paul is saying, "You think what I'm saying is new, but it's not. It's even older than the first covenant." Paul quotes Genesis 15:6, and surprise, here's the exact same expression he's been using since the first chapter. Here, *counted* or *credited* (NIV) has the same meaning as *from*, where righteousness is *from* God but given to *our* account as a gift. Note the economic or monetary language, for this is indeed a sort of a fiduciary or forensic reckoning. What counts is not what we do, but what God does, for we are not talking about wages paid by way of obligation. This is a hierarchical relationship where all credit goes to the superior agent, God. David is quoted from Psalm 32, pointing out that this is not a case of acquittal because of lack of evidence, but a case of pure mercy.

Referring to Abraham, Paul points out the sequence of events that puts the nail in the coffin of works righteousness. Righteousness was credited to him before he was circumcised, not after, making circumcision a physical or sacramental seal or sign of a prior and abiding spiritual reality. Just as we baptize infants who have no awareness or volitional role in their justification, we baptize all as a celebration of a prior forensic transaction whereby we are all justified without any contribution on our own part. The *ceremony* does nothing; it merely points to something that involved us even though we were not present. In fact, good sacramental ministry does not bring God to us, but rather takes us to God. We are taken back in time to the Cross whereby we realize that by that act we are justified; we were in effect *there*.[1] The sacrament erases time and shrinks distance. The Gentile who believes is then in the same place as Abraham, for neither was circumcised when they first believed. Jews who believe are also in debt to Abraham, whose faith they are called to emulate, without regard to the sign of Jewishness on their bodies.

13 For not through law
was the promise
to Abraham or his seed,
that he would be the heir of *the* world,
but through justfulness of faithfulness.
14 For if the heirs *are* from law,
null is *Abraham's* faithfulness
and void is *God's* promise,

1. Exod 13:8.

15 for the law produces vengeance. But where there is no law, neither transgression.

VV. 13–15

The NIV gives us *righteousness* in place of *justfulness*. *Promise* is a central theme in Paul's thoughts. Promises have to do with moral virtue. The agent who is virtuous makes promises and keeps them. Wedding vows, anyone? The whole idea of promise is antithetical to that of Law. Promise implies fulfillment regardless of performance, whereas Law implies fulfillment upon condition, condition that certain parameters are met. You can't mix the two; they are like oil and water. Oil and water cannot intersperse and dissolve because of a fundamental incompatibility in the valence of their atomic make-up. Paul is saying that Promise and Law are the same way; of such different conceptions that their intermingling is preposterous. They are separate and divorced because they are philosophically and congenitally incompatible.

Law brings wrath. Remember wrath? Wrath has to do with performance and expectation. What is the seat of anger but unmet expectations? Like with humans, so it is with God. When a person wants to reduce angst, increase communion, and mend breaches, what do they do? They lower their expectations of others. Specifically, they go to God and say, "How can I modify and ameliorate my reactions to others, without expectation of increased performance on their part?" So too, with diminished and more realistic expectations of Man, God is able to lower his standards and accept us as we are. With the cross, but apart from the Law, the wrath of God is expiated, and we stand a chance of being found lovable and salvable. Thanks be to God.

Paul again appeals to the historical record: the promises made to Abraham about his descendants were given at the time the first covenant was ratified in Genesis 15, not when the Law was given to Moses on Mount Sinai in Exodus 20. Sequence implies causality, just like in scientific inquiry. Who says spiritual revelation demands a suspension of credulity and logic? Science discusses process; theology discusses agency, intention, sequence, and import. What could be more important?

16 For this reason *the promise comes* from faithfulness,
in order that *it may come* as a gift,
so that the promise may be guaranteed to every seed,
not only to the *seed* from the law
but also to the *seed* from *the* faithfulness of Abraham,

who is father of us all 17 (as it is written: "Father of many nations I have made you")

in the sight of him in whom he had faith,

God, who gives life to the dead[23] and calls into being things that are not,

18 who against hope, in hope, had faith

that he would become "father of many nations," according to what was said, "So will your seed be."

19 And not weakening in faithfulness, he considered his own body as good as dead, being about a hundred years old, and the deadness of Sarah's womb.

20 But the promise of God

he did not doubt in unfaithfulness,

but he was strengthened in faithfulness,[24]

giving glory to God,

21 and being fully convinced that what *God* had promised he was also able to do.

22 That is why "it was counted to him as justfulness."

23 It was not written for him alone that "it was counted to him,"

24 but also for us, to whom it will be counted,

to those who put faith in him who raised Jesus our Lord from *the* dead,

25 who was handed over for our trespasses and raised for our justification.

[23] 4:17 *The dead.* Abraham and Sarah, verse 19, and Jesus, verse 24.

[24] 4:20 *Strengthened in faithfulness.* Paul suggests that Abraham's faith or faithfulness was an active partnership with God in fulfilling God's promise, based on the brief story in Gen 18–21. See also Gen 22:18.

God was not the only one who heard Sarah laugh when she heard God promise them a son (Gen 18:9–15; Rom 9:9). Abraham heard that laugh too and knew he had a part to do if God's promise was to be fulfilled. After the commotion died down from the destruction of Sodom, the home of Abraham's nephew, Lot, Abraham apparently persuaded 90-year-old Sarah to travel about 60 miles on camelback out of those dusty mountains for a vacation by the seaside. He probably encouraged her to get some new clothes for the occasion. Then, on the way, Abraham, the great warrior who didn't hesitate to wage war (Gen 14), became uncharacteristically timid and told Sarah of his fear that someone down there might be so attracted to her beauty that they might kill him to get her for a wife. He asked her to help save his life from a danger he was knowingly taking her into. And Sarah believed it. Sarah was beautiful, but she was 90 years

> old, and she had laughed at the thought of having sexual pleasure again (Gen 18:12). But her attitude was beginning to change.
>
> By the time they arrived, Sarah was glowing so much from Abraham's praise of her beauty, and looking so attractive in her new clothes, that the incredible happened. The King of Gerar noticed her and wanted her for his harem. Abraham played along by letting her go, saying he was only her brother. And God let her go through all the nuptial preparations at the palace before he rescued her. Nine months after Abraham and Sarah were reunited, Isaac ("He laughs") was born.
>
> Abraham's faithfulness was an active partnership with God to fulfill Abraham's greatest desire and God's promise, which neither could have done alone. The same can be said about Jesus' faithfulness (3:21–26).

VV. 16–25

Verse 16 is the conclusion of the chiasmus that began at verse 4:2b. The promise comes by faith, which implies grace, which is guaranteed. Grace, again, is Christ in us—a replacement, a substitution, a change of agency. When we're involved, the outcome is anything but guaranteed. When someone who is powerful and faithful is involved, however, then a guarantee becomes possible.

Hope. The word appears twice in rapid succession, yet in two different senses. The first use is as a synonym for logic, that which can be expected by dint of experience. The second use is not in reference to experience but as a synonym for faith, an expectation of divine intervention. Paul's whole point is that Abraham himself moved from unbelief to faith, and thus is a model for the progression Paul wants all Jews to make. There was indeed a time when Abraham's faith was weak, and he submitted to the idea that perhaps his descendants would be reckoned through his wife's maid Hagar. As we shall see later, this represents the temptation of fulfilling God's will through a shortcut of human contrivance. It was only after Abraham was given the seal of circumcision, however, that his faith in God's original promise was strengthened, and he was able to believe that he would have a child through Sarah. This is why God establishes sacraments: they are to focus our feeble faith and remind us of divine promises. Abraham was not perfect, and he shows that belief in God sometimes comes in steps, not all at once. We are in a hurry, God is not. He endures our errors, and forgives them, even when they have practical consequences later on. Sacraments, like circumcision under the first covenant, do not benefit God; they do not change God. They are for our benefit; they change us. They are a sign in the concrete world that there is another reality, a spiritual one, which will eventually supersede the physical realm and transform it.

Power (NIV). It all comes down to power: the power to promise, the power to believe, the power to wait. If it were easy, it would not justify God's valuation of our obedience. In Abraham's day, the struggle was over having a son. In Paul's day, the struggle was believing that God raised his son, Jesus, from the dead.

We are justified, accorded righteousness in a legal sense, because of the substitutionary atonement of Jesus Christ. Only. Paul described this atonement as a two-step process. Jesus was delivered over to death as a first step; he died in our place. But there's also a second part of the equation he mentions, that Jesus was also raised to life. As stated before, the resurrection was proof that Jesus' death on Good Friday was effective. By dying Jesus fulfilled the righteous demands of the Law, the Law that demands death as punishment. Having fulfilled those demands and submitted to the prescribed punishment, the Law itself was rendered irrelevant. It ceased to exist as a moral construct, and the punishment it imposed, death, was also removed. As of Good Friday, we are all justified in God's eyes; as of Easter Sunday, we are all justified in our own. We have been placed *in Christ* legally and offered proof that our faith might become knowledge. These are two sides of the same coin of our forensic acquittal: one divine, one human. God acts, and God also communicates the new reality to us.

Chapter 5

PRÉCIS

This chapter represents the beginning of a C section, the first of two, which extends from 5:1to 8:39. As such, the section constitutes a conclusion of all that was presented in the first four chapters. My summary title is "All are justified, those who live by the Spirit are also saved." This title reflects Paul's breakthrough revelation that justification, the forgiveness of sins, is separate and distinct from salvation, the impartation of the life of Jesus to us in the person of the Spirit. This understanding is central to developing an accurate and consistent soteriology.

In Anointed all are reconciled to God[25]

Justified through Anointed's faithfulness we are reconciled to God[26]

5 Justified therefore by *Anointed's* faithfulness, let us have peace[27] with God, through our Lord Jesus Anointed,

2 through whom also we have obtained access into this grace in which we stand,

and let us boast in hope of God's glory.

3 Not only *that*, but also let us boast in sufferings,

knowing that suffering produces endurance, 4 and endurance character, and character hope, 5 and hope does not disappoint,

because God's love has been poured out into our hearts through the holy spirit given to us.

6 For Anointed, while we were still weak, even then, he died for *the* godless.

7 Indeed, hardly for a just *person* will someone die,

though for a good *person* perhaps someone might even dare to die.

8 But God proves his love for us in that, while we were still sinners, Anointed died for us.

9 Much more then, being now justified by his blood,

will we be saved through him from *God's* vengeance.

10 For if, being enemies, we were reconciled to God through the death of his son,

much more, being reconciled,

will we be saved by his life.

11 Not only *that*, but also boasting[28] in God through our Lord Jesus Anointed through whom we have now received reconciliation.

[25] 5:1–8:39 ABCCBA. Parallel with 9:1—11:36.

[26] 5:1–11 ABA. Parallel with 8:9–39. The A's: our reconciliation with God. B: Anointed's faithfulness.

[27] 5:1 *Let us have peace* has far better manuscript support than the preferred reading of *we have peace*, (see Metzger's *A Textual Commentary on the Greek New Testament*, 1994) and is consistent with 5:2b–5, 6:12–23 and 12:1–2.

[28] 5:2,3,11 *Boast.* Boast or rejoice? The word translated "boast" here in verses 2, 3, and 11 is the same word usually translated "brag," "boast," or "pride" in 2:17,23; 3:27; and 4:2, where it refers to a Jew boasting of the law. Paul boasts here in God and sufferings rather than in the law and his own works.

VV. 1–2

It is my contention that chapters 5, 8, and 9 contain the most profound theological revelations ever made by the apostle, and that they are also the most misunderstood. Note Bailey's observation in footnote 25, that beginning with chapter 5 we have the first half of the conclusions of the entire document, which are themselves mirrored in chapter 9, both C sections. All that has gone before is preliminary, and what follows through the end of chapter 9 is central.

Chapter divisions in the Bible were imposed long after the books were written, and they reflect almost nothing of the author's intent. Thus, the first sentence of this chapter is actually a continuation of the thought expressed in the last sentence of chapter 4. *Justified through faith* (NIV) or *by Anointed's faithfulness.* The latter rendering opens up whole new vistas of meaning. We are not justified because we have faith, as evangelicals teach, but we are justified because of what Jesus did: his faithfulness in executing the call which he received at his baptism. At that time, he submitted to being identified with mankind's sins, and our justification was actualized on the Cross. Paul is always stressing faith as a response to God's sovereign action, not because our faith somehow enables justification, but because faith stands in opposition to works for Jews and license for Gentiles. Many a commentator has stumbled over this fact. Our faith does nothing to move human justification forward. Our justification is a *fait accompli* that does not in any way depend upon human awareness or response.[1] It's as if Paul were saying *through faith* as a negation, not a positive qualification—faith as opposed to works. It's not as though justification requires faith to take place, faith simply reveals to human perception what has already taken place on earth and in heaven.

Peace with God. We're justified by Christ's death, we received validation of this happy state through His resurrection, and we now have peace with God as a result. The prior mutual enmity that existed between God and us has been demolished by Christ's obedience to his father in going to the Cross. Ever since Genesis 3:6, God has been at odds with Man, and Man has been at odds with God. The communion that was displayed by mutual walks in the Garden could no longer take place. The metaphor of nakedness speaks of our experiential guilt for being at odds with God. *Standing in Grace.* A cup that is dirty is washed before it is used. The human must be washed clean before he can withstand the habitation of the Son of God in the person of the Holy Spirit. We have been placed *in Christ* legally as of Good Friday. Christ has in potential been placed *in us* effectually as of Pentecost. This mutual interpenetration constitutes a reestablishment of the spiritual reality that was God's intent in the Garden of Eden. We had been separated from the glory of God; now it's our sure and certain heritage in heaven.

V. 3

We are not, however, in heaven at present. In the meantime, we suffer because the world is fallen, and it resists God's plan of redemption. The irony of human rebellion is that we curse and resist the very means that have been graciously provided for our restoration. Our lustful bodies and carnal

1. See Donald Bloesch: "Something happened for our salvation in the death and resurrection of Jesus Christ independent of our belief or response. Reconciliation and redemption are an accomplished fact, an objective reality that is not affected by the subjective attitude of man. . . . The atonement of Jesus Christ signifies a transformation of the human situation, and not simply the possibility of a future salvation." Bloesch, *God, Authority & Salvation,* 162.

minds resent their dethronement and subjugation to the newly revitalized Spirit who has been imparted to us, and they conspire to take us back to the Egypt of base living where they reigned unopposed.

God's revelation is not just about eternal promises, but about promises that will find fulfillment in *this* life. Proper worship bears fruit here and now, not just when we die. Paul lays out a mechanism by which something bad, suffering, actually bears fruit that is good. This is not a celebration of asceticism *per se*. Christianity is not religion of self-denial; it does not teach that the created order is bad, as do ascetic religions like Buddhism, Hinduism, or Gnosticism.

V. 4

This is a sequence of spiritual growth that the father wants all his children to go through. Nobody chooses suffering, but it befalls one and all. The question is not, will bad things happen to us, but rather, how will we react to the bad that is sure to come? Will it result in our perseverance or our capitulation regarding our spiritual heritage? Will people accuse God of being lax in terms of protecting us and curse his name as Job's wife suggested?[2] None of these steps is optional; all are necessary. The order is also sacrosanct. It can be said there are two types of people in the world: those who allow themselves to go through this process and those who refuse. The former are successful in God's eyes; the latter are not. God surrounds himself with people of character. People lacking character are described as being empty kernels, chaff. Note what this process omits: blessings. Blessings, as Agur points out, tend to make us forget God.[3] This is the crime of prosperity Christianity, for it teaches that God wants to deliver righteous people from suffering while withholding blessings from the errant. Such nonsense keeps people from learning through life's vicissitudes that they should persevere and develop character. This is God's permissive will in action.

V. 5

Hope. The firm belief that the present circumstances do not constitute the final situation, but that better will prevail. One role of the Holy Spirit is to serve as a down payment, a foretaste of God and heaven that will sustain us while we yet struggle in this world.

2. Job 2:9.
3. Prov 30:9.

The Holy Spirit given to us, the Holy Spirit, whom he has given us (NIV). The Greek source presents *of being given* or *having been given* in the genitive form, suggesting the necessity of a determiner pronoun tying the verb *given* to its object, *the Holy Spirit*. Bailey offers a minimalist translation that does not take this into account, whereas most published translations do. The words for *ghost* and its definite article are neuter and singular, allowing the KJV to offer *which*. The NIV gives us *the Holy Spirit whom* and the New American Standard Bible offers *the Holy Spirit who*. These interpolations suggest the Holy Spirit is a person, nothing less than the Spirit of Jesus himself. A third, concurring interpretation from Bible Hub suggests *the*, definite article, and *(One)* in parentheses, as having been given, understanding personality or individuality.[4] Although not demanded by the Greek, I favor those interpretations that ascribe "having an implication of personality"[5] to the Holy Spirit in this context.

VV. 6–8

Even then or *just the right time* (NIV). Paul speaks elsewhere of the fullness of time. In historical terms, this was the Pax Romana, when the known world possessed dependable travel, communication, and political stability.[6] Here, however, Paul is addressing his audience imploring action after the Fall, while we live, and before we die—in other words, *now*.[7] This is a golden period of mercy designed to lead us to repentance, as already stated.

Powerless (NIV) or *weak*. This is the second great problem of Man. Guilt is the first; powerlessness is the second.[8] We can know what to do or not do, it's just that we can't make our actions conform to our moral perceptions.

Godless or *ungodly* (NIV). Paul never misses a chance to skewer the Jews who think they're godly. Christ's death was completely unmerited by human virtue and is strictly the result of God having mercy on his errant children, and not only the errant, but also those deliberately hostile to him.

4. Bible Hub, "Romans 5:5," line 2.
5. Brown, *SOED*, "whom, n. 2," 3679.
6. Gal 4:4.
7. 2 Cor 6:2.
8. Rom 7.

VV. 9–11

These verses are the crux of Pauline soteriology. It is commentators' collective inability to understand these three verses that has led to all the schisms, arguments, confusion, denominational fragmentation, and the current anemia in the Christian church. The confusion revolves around this seeming paradox: how can Jesus die for the sins of the whole world,[9] yet not all are redeemed.[10] The various communions, denominations, and Christian sects have their own answers as to how the benefits of the Cross are available to some but not all. Depending on the group consulted, you will be told that the answer involves divine fiat, church membership, sacramental practice engendering justification, cooperating with proffered grace, or merely knowledge of divine history. It is a goal of this commentary to provide a simple, correct answer to this divisive question.

Let me be clear: Paul does not use terms loosely. He does, as all Biblical authors do, employ figures of speech, metaphors, and symbolic language. However, he is not casual in his choice of words or in the structure of his arguments. In this specific instance, he uses the term *justify* or *justification*, which he has already used eight times in some form. He then contrasts it with a new and utterly different concept, *salvation*, something he's only mentioned once before. He makes this distinction because they are two different theological constructs. Specifically, the one, justification, is an act of God that does not involve human agency to any degree. Further, justification is logically prior to, and a prerequisite for, salvation. At this point, it is helpful to divide God's plan of redemption, the mechanism of salvation, into three parts. The first part focuses on how God engineers our justification.

Table 1. How We Are Justified

Actor	Man's Problem	Attitude as of the Fall	Solution	Judgment	Extent
God	Guilt	Enmity with Man	Blood of Christ	On Sin	Universal

There are two moral actors in the drama of creation, God and Man. But our justification is engineered by God alone without any human involvement. As such, it is referred to as monergistic. To deal with our guilt, God ordains that Jesus lead a sinless life then die a sinner at our hands. This is the first judgment on Sin and sins, both the disposition and the actual

9. 1 John 2:2.

10. Matt 7:14; Luke 13:24.

deeds. As of Good Friday, all humanity, past, present, and future, stands justified and righteous in God's sight. Our sins will never again come between God and us. As with the rainbow after the Flood, God promises to no longer pass destructive judgment on all mankind. This is the ascribed righteousness that allowed Luther to say he felt born again and able to enter paradise.[11]

Table 2. How We Can Be Saved

Actor	Man's Problem	Attitude as of the Fall	Solution	Judgment	Extent
God/Man	Powerless-ness	Our Enmity with God	Life of Christ	On Fruit-lessness	Particular

In addition to moral guilt, however, we have a second problem: we are powerless to reform. This is because our spirit, as of the Fall, is so attenuated, injured, and destroyed that, though forgiven, we persist in spiritual independence and consequent sinful acts. Whereas the *blood* of Jesus was the key to solving our first problem, the *life* of Jesus, as Paul says here, is the solution to solving our second. There is a second judgment, pending at least for the living, not for sins but for fruitlessness. Note that in the two accounts of the final judgment found in the New Testament, neither mentions positive sins.[12] Rather, they mention the absence of good deeds.[13] The Book of Life records those in whom the *life* of Christ dwells, rendering them capable of doing good. Thus, according to Paul, it's perfectly possible to be justified, which is a universal ascription for all born human,[14] yet be found wanting on the final day when we are judged according to the extent to which the life of Jesus was in us bearing fruit. Jesus himself says that the fruitless branches that are cut off and burned were originally *in me*.[15] Failure at this latter judgment renders justification nugatory. In fact, *wrath* is the best description of God's attitude towards those who may well accept Jesus as Savior, but who refuse to obey him as Lord.[16] Thus, we cannot justify ourselves, but we *can*

11. Luther, *Luther's Works*, 336–337.

12. Matt 25:31–46; Rev 20:11–15.

13. Jas 4:17.

14. Oswald Chambers writes, "... we are condemned to salvation." Chambers often uses salvation the way I use justification. Chambers, *My Utmost*, February 2.

15. John 15:2.

16. Matt 7:21–23. Scripture abounds with testimony that man's primary problem is not with legal rectitude but actual behavior. The Jewish sacramental system provided for atonement, at least temporarily, but it could not engender obedience. See

interfere with God's efforts to save us. As such, our salvation involves two actors: God and man. The initiative lies with the father and the son, but playing host to the Holy Spirit requires that we cede our wills. This is a disposition that involves our knowledge, consent, and cooperation. Salvation is therefore said to by synergistic.

Table 3. Christian Faith and Practice

Position Relative to Christ	Sacrament	Historic Event	Role of Christ	Theological Term
We in Christ legally	Baptism	Good Friday	Savior	Justification
Christ in us effectually	Eucharist	Pentecost	Lord	Salvation

We come finally to how we perceive and participate in God's plan of redemption, as portrayed in Table 3. Good preaching tells us that in addition to being in Christ in a legal sense, Christ must also be in us in a practical sense, in the person of his Spirit. We celebrate our justification in baptism, agreeing our will should be crucified as Jesus was. This negation of our will finds expression in penitence and humility. Baptism is to take us back to the Cross and tell us that in a very real way, we were there. We nailed Jesus to the cross ourselves. Because he took the punishment we deserved, we accord him honor as our Savior, and we rejoice that we stand justified in the father's eyes.

Now that we've heard the one sermon Baptists know how to preach, we must stay in church and hear the next sermon, which addresses our second problem: powerlessness.[17] And not only should we hear this accurate catechesis, we should also proceed to the altar rail and apply it to ourselves. This is the purpose of the Eucharist, that we should ask Jesus to nourish his Spirit in us in the same way our bodies require repeated nourishment from bread and wine. Altar calls are not a one-time affair; it is said of the apostles that they were repeatedly filled with the Holy Spirit. Each of us must have an ongoing Pentecostal experience wherein we allow the Spirit of Jesus to reform our mind and thereby gain control over our body.

The exact nature of this experience varies and must not be codified according to one's personal experience. However, all encounters with the Holy

Lev 26:3–13; 1 Sam 15:22–23; Ps 40:6–8; 50:8–23; 51:16–17; Prov 21:3; Isa 1:11–20; 58; 66:2–4; Jer 6:20; 7:21–26; Hos 6:6; Amos 4:4; 5:25; Mic 6:6–8; Zech 7:8–10; Matt 12:7; 1 Cor 7:19; Heb 10:8.

17. Heb 6:1–3.

Spirit share the following three markers. First, there is a profound sense of conviction of sin. Second, there is a revelation of the power and accuracy of Holy Scripture. And finally, there is an unbridled joy at being alive as a three-part person, as we were in the Garden. There are many names for this experience: baptism in the Holy Spirit, new birth, regeneration, sanctification, etc. Whatever term we choose, we're talking about being overmastered by the Spirit of Jesus, whom we defer to and obey as Lord.[18]

It's about authority—his, not ours. This is why the only unforgiveable sin is blaspheming the Holy Spirit, and it's why Jesus forgives all sins against himself but not against his distributed Spirit.[19] Note: the Spirit authored the Bible, and thus to disobey its plain sense is another form of blasphemy against him. The Spirit is given freely, but God respects our free will and will not insist on our obedience. To argue with the Spirit is to recommit Adam's sin and nail Jesus to the Cross all over again.[20]

The relevant verses upon which this argument is based are, as stated, 5:9–11. In contrast to Bailey, I would portray the symmetrical parallelism in the form of ABABA, where the A verses refer to justification, and the B verses to salvation.

A) 9 Much more then, being now justified by his blood,

B) will we be saved through him from *God's* vengeance

A) 10 For if, being enemies, we were reconciled to God through the death of his son, much more, being reconciled,

B) will we be saved by his life.

A) 11Not only *that*, but also boasting in God through our Lord Jesus Anointed through whom we have now received reconciliation.

Note that the end result of submitting to God's plan of redemption is that we can fully *rejoice* (NIV) or *boast*. Good theology, in this case, good soteriology, leads to worship.

As the sin of one reigned in death to all, grace reigns in life through one, Jesus[29]

12 Therefore, as through one man sin entered into the world, and through sin death,

and so to all came death, in that all sinned.

13 For until law,

sin was in *the* world,

18. Gal 4:6; 1 Peter 1:11.

19. Mark 3:28–29; Luke 12:10.

20. Col 2:14.

but sin is not counted

when there is no law.

14 But death reigned from Adam to Moses,

even over those who did not sin after the likeness of the transgression of Adam, who is a type of the one to come.

15 But not as the trespass, so also *is* the gift.

For if through the trespass of the one, the many died,

much more the grace of God and the gift by the grace of the one man, Jesus Anointed, to the many has overflowed.

16 And not as by *the* sinning of one *is* the gift.

For the judgment *came* out of *the sinning of* one into condemnation,

but the gift *comes* out of the trespasses of many into justfulness.

17 For if

by the trespass of the one,

death reigned

through the one,

much more

they who receive the abundance of the grace and of the gift of justfulness,

in life will reign

through the one, Jesus Anointed.

18 So then as

by *the* trespass of one,

judgment came to all for condemnation,

so also

by *the* justifying act of one,

the gift comes to all for justfulness of life.

19 For as

by the disobedience of the one man,

the many were made sinners,

so also

by the obedience of the one,

the many will be made just.

20 Law entered in
so that trespassing might increase.
But where sin increased,
grace increased much more,
21 so that as
reigned sin
in death,
so also
grace may reign
through justfulness into eternal life
through Jesus Anointed our Lord.

[29] 5:12–21 ABA: 12–14, 15–16, 17–21. Parallel with 7:1—8:8.

VV. 12–21

Note Bailey's brief chiasmus. Adam sinned, and in his separation from God there was death. Vegetarians will rejoice that in the Garden there is no record of eating meat; until the Fall, even animals were apparently spared death. Yet because we are Adam's descendants, we all carry in our spiritual DNA both the cause and consequences of the Fall.

The term original sin is not found in Scripture as such, but starting with Augustine and continuing in Western thought through Aquinas, its existence has been surmised from, to a large degree, verse 12. Dogma about Mary as *theotokos* and her own immaculate conception are based upon viewing original sin as a positive construct, something we caught from Adam, like the flu. Aquinas says "…contract the infection…" My contention is that it is not something positive, but rather negative, a lack. I base this on Genesis 3:23,24, where expulsion from the Garden and God's presence represents deprivation of spiritual capacity.

Before the Law (NIV) or *until law*. The Bible bears consistent witness to gradations of reward and punishment, and this is just one example. Elsewhere, it is said those who know better will be judged more strictly than those who sin unawares.[21] The Jews thought the Law was an unadulterated blessing. It was a blessing, to be sure, but it was also a heavy responsibility. Knowledge of the moral demands of God, to say nothing of the ceremonial demands, precludes any claims of ignorance. Before the Jews came along, God tolerated sin to a large degree. Yet even though God was not holding

21. Mark 12:40; Luke 12:47–48.

Man to a perfect standard in terms of judgment, Man nevertheless was subject to the punishment reserved for Adam in this life, and that is physical death. It's been said that we can always serve as a bad example, and this is what Adam did. Yet even in his stupidity and rebellion, Adam prefigures Jesus. God is fond of doing things twice. He does them once—in historical time, imperfectly, and temporarily. He then does them a second time—spiritually, permanently, and perfectly. Just as sin entered the world through one man, it will also, in potential, be eradicated by one man, the Son of Man.

Much more. This is a consistent theme of Paul's; he uses the phrase five times in this letter alone. He wishes to amplify the fact that God is merciful beyond any measure of justice or probity. What he does is far beyond what we can ask or imagine. What we have done wrong is out of all proportion to reason, yet God's plan of redemption knows no limits. *Receive.* We can frustrate God's plan by refusing to receive something. There is a role for us, but it's negative. We must make room for God's plan without argument, shortcut, substitution, or emendation. Note how he's still keeping Grace, Christ in us, separate from the gift of righteousness, which is justification, we in Christ. Physical death still obtains, but it's a mere speed bump for the Christian. In heaven we will reign in life with Christ.

I am reminded of Jesus' baptism, where his vocation of identifying with the sins of humanity was confirmed by God's voice and Spirit. Further, when Jesus was glorified on the Mount of Transfiguration, he refused that rightful glory and immediate entrance into heaven, instead choosing to go to the Cross. And in the Garden of Gethsemane, he accepts the father's will that he not waver in that vocation. Jesus didn't come to teach; he came to die. The Son of God becomes the Son of Man, our true representative.

The Law wasn't given that it might be obeyed. It was given to impart knowledge of Sin to us, and to vindicate God's judgment on human trespass. But God is not content to merely expose Sin. He exposes Sin that it might be recognized and dealt with, and with finality. *Grace might reign through righteousness* (NIV) or *Grace may reign through justfulness.* Grace is Christ in us, and it's possible because we are accounted righteous, we in Christ. The happy result? *Eternal life.* Heaven is not a continual, unending church service. God is indeed outside of time, and the ticking clock of *chronos* is not found in heaven. It has been said that when you don't have a schedule, you can't be late. As the bride of Christ, the church will be his partner in the administration of a new heaven and earth where there is no sin or dissent, and all agree that Jesus is Lord.

Chapter 6

PRÉCIS

Earlier chapters find Paul dismantling the specious arguments of both Jew and Gentile as to why they don't need Christ. In this chapter, Paul squares off against a new adversary, namely Christian antinomians who say that our justification renders behavior irrelevant. Today's church is beset with schisms caused by the resurrection of these same "progressive" arguments. Paul's response has lost none of its relevance to our current plight.

We died to sin with Anointed so we may live with him in his resurrection[30]

6 What then shall we say?
Should we persist
in sin
that grace
may increase?
2 Not at all!
We who died to sin, how can we still live in it?
3 Or do you not know that we who were baptized
into Anointed Jesus,
into his death
we were baptized?
4 We were buried with him by baptism into death,
so that, as Anointed was raised from *the* dead by the Father's glory,
so we too in newness of life may walk.

5 For if we have been united
in the likeness of his death,
then also *in the likeness* of *his* resurrection
we will be *united*,
6 knowing this, that our old self
was crucified with *him*
so that done away with may be
the body of sin,
so that we should no longer be enslaved to sin.
7 For one who has died
is justified from sin.
8 If, then, we have died with Anointed,
we believe that we will also live with him,
9 knowing that Anointed,
being raised from *the* dead,
dies no more, death no longer is lord over him.
10 The *death* he died,
to sin he died, once,
but the *life* he lives,
he lives to God.
11 So you also must think of yourselves
as dead to sin
and living for God
in Anointed Jesus.
12 Therefore do not let sin reign in your mortal body, to obey its desires.
13 Do not give your members as instruments of evil to sin,
but give yourselves to God as alive from *the* dead,
and your members as instruments of justfulness to God.
14 For sin will not be lord over you, since you are not under law but under grace.

[30]6:1–14 ABBA. Parallel with 6:15–23. Answers to question in 6:1 (and in 3:8.)

VV. 1–5

Paul now turns from the Jews to heckle once again the antinomians who construe freedom in Christ as license. If Christ freely forgives, then why not sin with impunity? This was a good question then, and it is a good question today. Paul argues that these people fail to take into account the fact that when we are born from above, sin no longer has any allure. The Cross was significant for two reasons. First of all, Jesus took the sins of the world upon himself and paid the penalty those sins demanded: death. As such, it was a forensic event that involved him directly and us indirectly. But Paul argues that there's a second aspect to the Cross that involves us directly. Baptism is a symbol of death, a burial with water as opposed to dirt, as water's easier to clean up from. It is a burial, nonetheless. Good sacramental theology shows that each sacrament has two sides: a God side and a human side. In the case of baptism, the God side is that by virtue of the Cross, we are placed in Christ. The man side is that we, too, are crucified as was Jesus. Baptism should be understood as celebrating the death of Christ, a cosmic event, and also creating a metaphor for the death of our individual wills as we come to appreciate the relevance of his sacrifice. Put another way, just as Jesus submitted his will to his father's and went to a painful death on the Cross, we too, must submit our will to Jesus and put to death all individual claims and aspirations of our own. The Cross is universal in a legal sense, and also particular in a moral sense. It offers comfort in that our sins are forgiven, but it also issues a challenge. While we yet live, we are to bury our will, as signified in baptism, and rise to a new life under the direction of the living Jesus who is now our Lord. The Cross of Christ is also a cross of the individual, upon which we must hang all that is not of God, all that went before. We cannot have new life until we let go of the old. To cling to the old while the prospect of a new life is available is lunacy to Paul, and for good reason.

VV. 6–7

The body of sin. When we are unregenerate, our spirit lies fallow, and our body dominates our thinking. A body in charge is necessarily a body of sin, for its appetites and desires will find expression without regard to morality or probity. This body must be re-subjugated to control by the mind, itself controlled by a revitalized spirit.

When someone tells me they want to die, that they want to kill themselves, I respond that this is a common problem. We are supposed to die, but in a spiritual, not literal, way. Apart from Christ our lives do indeed breed *ennui*. What's the point? We wake up to fulfill our carnal desires, we drape our actions with the semblance of rationality and morality, yet satisfaction escapes us at every turn. What is more important than the search for significance? Nothing, I posit. Yet what is significant about fulfilling our base desires day after day, with no higher purpose? When we allow ourselves to die in a spiritual sense, where we go through what Oswald Chambers calls a "white funeral,"[1] we embark on a spiritual path that God intends all his children take. First of all, the dead man has no sensation of pain. He becomes insensate to that which assaulted him before. Grievances, hurts, debit accounts with others—all this falls away when one dies. Further, we move beyond the reach of Sin. When we were Adam's child, Sin, the disposition of our right to ourselves, was a harsh taskmaster. When we died to self, however, we moved from being Adam's child, with all that implies, to being a new creature, a new child, now of God. The ruling disposition that was passed from Adam through all the generations to us, perfectly intact, has been displaced, and a new disposition has been substituted. This disposition does not immediately rebel and seek justification for itself. Rather, it's a new spiritual constitution, manifesting obedience and trust. We are born again.

VV. 8–10

Whatever happened to Christ happens to us. He died; we die. He was raised to new life; we, too, are raised to new life. And not just any life, we are raised to a new life that is inviolable, in spite of our lingering physical mortality. When Jesus died, he defeated death; the Law was fulfilled, and the penalty, death, was annulled. This is a one-time, forensic event, presaged by the sacrificial practices of the Jews, but now fulfilled once and for all. Having been obedient to the father's will, Jesus was raised to life, and the glory he had given up has been restored to him. He is now authorized to share that new life with us through his Spirit.

VV. 11–14

Think of yourselves or *count yourselves* (NIV). It's not enough that something *is*, we have to know that it *is* in a way that leads to decision and action. Again, this contrasts the Eastern view of belief with the Western view. The importance of behavior is now brought out, because behavior not only determines our receptivity to the guidance of the Holy Spirit, but it also reveals our character. Do we have a mercenary approach to our Lord, where we worship as long as we get some benefit? Are we like the Jews, lusting after the fleshpots of Egypt and wishing for the indulgences of our prior life? Do we really hate our former life of sin, or did we just resent the consequences?

1. Chambers, *My Utmost*, January 15.

Are we hanging on because we have genuine hope for the future, or are we just afraid of falling off? It all comes down to Lordship. Sin is the harshest taskmaster, for its author and guide is the Devil. We will be servant to somebody. Will it be somebody who loves us and wants us to succeed? Or will it be somebody who hates us, who wants us to fail, who wants us to suffer now in this life, and who especially wants us to suffer torment for eternity? The Devil's number one accusation is that the life in Christ will be dull, lacking, insecure, and difficult. It's anything but; that's a better description of life under Law. The life of Grace is a life of relief, rest, confidence, and hope. Somebody else is doing the hard work; our job is simply to make ourselves available for a great adventure that unfolds one day at a time.

Being freed from sin, be slaves to God in Anointed Jesus[31]

15 What then? Should we sin because we are not under law but under grace?

Not at all!

16 Do you not know that to whom you offer yourselves as slaves for obedience,

you are slaves to whom you obey,

either of sin into death, or of obedience into justfulness?

17 But thanks to God,

you were slaves of sin, but you have obeyed from *the* heart the pattern of teaching to which you were handed over.

18 And having been freed from sin,

you have been enslaved to justfulness.

19 I am speaking in human terms because of the weakness of your flesh. For just as you offered your members as slaves to impurity and to lawlessness for lawlessness,

so now offer your members as slaves to justfulness for holiness.

20 For when you were slaves of sin,

you were free from justfulness.

21 So what fruit did you have then in the *things* you are now ashamed of?

For the end of those *is* death.

22 But now, having been freed from sin and enslaved to God,

you have your fruit for holiness, and the end *is* eternal life.

23 For sin's pay *is* death,

but God's gift *is* eternal life in Anointed Jesus our Lord.

[31] 6:15–23 ABA. Respond to God's gift in Anointed, that is, respond to faithfulness with faithfulness.

VV. 15–18

Sins are not just events, things we do that remain outside ourselves. They are also invitations issued in the spirit world, and demons are ready to accept those invitations at the earliest opportunity. Whenever we sin by exhibiting inordinate affection for alcohol, pharmaceuticals, money, prestige, physical attributes, sexual pleasure, revenge, or unforgiveness, we are worshipping that entity. Demons love worship and have been instructed to not return home until they have wrought damage on the one offering them worship.[2] We offer worship through sins, then come under the dominion of those very forces that we invited in. Once the invitation is issued, the tables are turned, and we lose any control we initially had. Sin leads to death, both physically and spiritually. The body was not designed for abuse, and neither is the soul. By worshipping amiss, we invite degeneration in both realms. The only solution to spiritual bondage is repentance, where we turn around and obey correct teaching. Obedience is the conformance of the mind to new spiritual revelation, and the domination of the body by a mind that has thereby been renewed. We will all be a slave to somebody, the question is, to whom?

VV. 19–22

To impurity and to lawlessness for lawlessness or *ever-increasing wickedness* (NIV). Sin has a threshold, and that threshold is constantly moving upward. That which satisfied at first is no longer capable of bringing satisfaction, and we are rendered more and more powerless to resist the call of Sin.

Holiness. It is a byproduct of an inner slavery to righteousness. How we worship and where we derive our self-image, this is what determines how we behave. Wrong behavior is a sign of spiritual independence, while holiness is a sign of dependence upon God. *Now ashamed of.* Ashamed indeed. The Devil delights in making his servants do degrading things. Sexual sins, for example, are his preferred method of removing dignity and innocence. Where is shame? What used to be kept secret is now out in the open, flaunted, celebrated, and laughed at. *End of those is death* or *Result in death* (NIV). Note how God is always raising up penalties for wrong behavior.

2. Matt 8; Mark 5; Luke 8.

Venereal disease, certain cancers, starvation, divorce—these things are not God's deliberate will, but part of his permissive will that those experiencing the consequences of sin might come to their right mind and repent. These maladies result in physical death both as part of the Devil's desire to kill, steal, and destroy, and as part of God's desire that we witness what life looks like apart from his Grace.

V. 23

Sin's pay or *wages of sin* (NIV). Note how righteousness is not given as a wage or obligation, but as a gift. The economy of sin, however, is still paying those wages, the obligations. Which sort of economy do we want to work under? One where we get what we deserve, or one where we get better than we deserve? The choice is ours.

Death. There are two deaths. Adam died when he was expelled from the Garden and suffered death in his spirit. The second is when we each die physically, and we become subject to judgment on whether or not the Life of Christ is in us. There are two lives, as well. The life that was ours when we were physically born, and then the life we each received when our Spirit is brought back to life in our personal Pentecost.[3] It's that life, the life of Jesus that lives in us, that continues through physical death and is released into the new dimension of Heaven when we die. Eternal doesn't mean long, it means beyond the bounds of time.

3. John 3:5–6.

Chapter 7

PRÉCIS

Here Paul turns his attention back to the Jews in his audience, who believe that knowledge of God's requirements, as embodied in the Law, is sufficient to allow successful living. He deals with the seeming contradiction that something good, the Law, can actually be bad if we do not recognize its limitations. One of the primary functions of the Law is to impart an awareness of Sin.

Freed from the law of sin and death by the law of the spirit of life in Anointed[32]

7 Do you not know, brothers,
for to those who know law
I am speaking,
that the law is binding over one
only for as long as one lives?
2 Thus the married woman to the living husband is bound by law,
but if the husband dies, she is released from the law of the husband.
3 So then, the husband living, adulteress she will be called if she goes to another man,
but if the husband dies, she is free from that law,
and she is not an adulteress if she goes to another man.
4 So, my brothers, you also have been put to death to the law
through the body of the Anointed,
so that you may belong to another,

to him who was raised from the dead,
in order that we may bear fruit for God.
5 For when we were in the flesh, the passions of sins, those through the law, worked in our members
to bear fruit for death.
6 But now we are released from the law, having died to what was binding *us*,
so we may serve in newness of spirit and not oldness of letter.

[32] 7:1—8:8 ABCBA. 7:1–6 and 8:1–8: freed from the law of sin and death to serve God in the spirit of life in Anointed Jesus; 7:7–13 and 24–25 describe the futility of rescuing ourselves; 7:14–23: God's law is good but we are captive to the law of sin; 7:7—8:8 is a dialogue conducted in the singular "I" and singular "you."

VV. 1–4

Belong to another, or be married to another (KJV.) The Greek is *ginomai*, a diverse term that implies a change of status. Francis Schaeffer is unparalleled here: "The Bible tells us plainly that Christ promises to bear His fruit through us. . . . This verse says that each of us as a Christian is feminine. At conversion we are married to Christ, who is the bridegroom, and as we put ourselves in his arms, moment by moment, he will produce His fruit through us into the external world. That is beautiful and overwhelming. Just as with the natural bride who gives herself to her husband and puts herself in his arms, there will be children born into a home. The bride can't just stand with the bridegroom at the wedding ceremony. She must give herself to him existentially, regularly and then children will be born to him, through her body, into the external world."[1] This insight may explain why men seem to be more obtuse and slow to recognize the claims of Christ in their lives. Those who are habituated to the role of initiator may find it awkward to be placed in the role of responder.

It also explains why the ordination of women to sacramental ministry might interfere with this moral transaction between the worshiper and Christ. In 1991 J. I. Packer presented several cogent arguments that inveighed against the practice, one of which was as follows: "To minimize the maleness of Christ shows a degree of failure to grasp the space-time reality and redemptive significance of the Incarnation; to argue that gender is irrelevant to ministry shows that one is forgetting the representative role of presbyteral leadership."[2] C. S. Lewis, in his 1948 essay "Priestesses in the

1. Schaeffer, *The Universe and Two Chairs*, 294.
2. Packer, *Christianity Today*, 20.

Church?," elaborates upon what Jesus might expect from this bride. Lewis says that in liturgical worship involving ordained ministers, there are times when the minister faces liturgical East and speaks to God on behalf of the people. There are other times where he turns around and, facing the people, speaks to them on behalf of God. Lewis argues that in this latter situation, the minister must be male to represent Christ who is addressing his bride, the Church.[3] The Bible abounds with references to the spiritual interplay between God and man as having sexual and gender overtones. The sexualization and feminization of worship apart from the Messiah was always a snare to the Jews, and if Packer, Schaeffer and Lewis are correct, sexual and romantic symbolism is being abused by the ordination of women. To have a female performing sacramental ritual is to lose the romantic aspect of our relationship with our Lord and Savior, and thereby miss his invitation to cede our will to him. The ordination of only men to the priesthood and the episcopate shows that church discipline is not an end in itself, but a means to an end. By being careful about received tradition, we might unwittingly protect spiritual truth that outweighs cultural relevance.

VV. 5–6

The Law not only corrupts our relationship with God, suggesting that we might somehow fulfill its regulations, but it also corrupts our relations with each other. It gives us the notion that we have rights, and that we can expect others to respect those rights. When they fail to do so, we can claim unmet expectations and be at enmity with them. This is the way of the world. As good as this feels, the advantages of giving up our rights are manifold. When we renounce our right to ourselves, when we forget all the outrages that have been committed against us and ours over the years, when we give up our right to be treated fairly and to retaliate in kind, we are in effect dead. We are no longer concerned with the past: our race, our family, our heritage, our gifts, our handicaps. When we identify with Christ's death, we become free to identify with his interests in others. How can we serve them in the here and now so that Christ's life and Lordship might be made manifest to them?[4] Our concern focuses on the future and potential progress, not recriminations.

> [**Teacher of Law**[33]] 7 What then should we say? The law *is* sin? Not at all!
> But sin I did not know
> except through law,

3. Lewis, *God in the Dock*, 120.
4. Col 1:24.

and desire I had not known
except the law said, "Do not desire."
8 But sin, taking opportunity through the commandment,
produced in me every desire,
for apart from law sin *is* dead.
9 I was alive apart from law formerly,
but when came the commandment,
sin came to life,
10 and I died
and I found the commandment
that *was* for life *to be* for death.
11 For sin, taking opportunity through the commandment,
deceived me
and through it killed *me.*
12 So the law *is* holy, and the commandment holy and just and good.
13 Then the good to me became death? Not at all!
But sin, so that it may be shown to be sin,
through the good to me worked death,
so that sin may become utterly sinful through the commandment.

33 7:7–25 *Teacher of Law.* This person is both the Gentile Judge of 2:1–16 and the Jewish Teacher of 2:17—4:2.

VV. 7–12

Is the law Sin? (NIV) I use a capital letter here because in this instance Paul is dealing with the inner disposition of Sin, as opposed to the individual incidents of rebellion that are considered sinful, and therefore sins. Sin to Paul is a technical term, not some vague notion. Sin takes on an animate nature in these verses, because in a very real way, Sin is the tool, the mechanism of the Devil, to turn us to his purposes. The metaphor that appears in the Scriptures is eating from the tree of the knowledge of Good and Evil. Namely, it is Sin that tells us that we are able to decide what is good and what is evil; we are our own moral standard. This is what Paul's getting at when he says Sin sprang to life. To the extent that Sin is personal, creative, variable, and adaptable, it is alive.

Deceived me. Adam and Eve were deceived. They were told something that was untrue, or only partly true, and chose to believe it over the command they had received from God. When we try to obey the Law, we fail, and we have two choices. Either we try harder, and become hypocrites, or we give up, and become irreligious. The honest person knows that either way leads to failure and damnation.

V. 13

Sin . . . shown to be sin or *Sin might be recognized as sin* (NIV). Man can deal with individual sins, to the extent he is motivated. What he can't deal with, however, is Sin, which is the overarching disposition to decide for himself what's right or wrong. We are incapable of receiving a command based on Law and not resenting its intrusion, its interference with our independence. The real purpose of the Law is not that we obey it, but that we try to obey it, fail, and then realize that there's something desperately wrong with us about which we can do nothing. Just like the experience of the Jewish people, all this is intended by God to teach us something about our moral incapacity. We're not supposed to succeed, we're supposed to fail and come to a startling conclusion about ourselves. Like the Jews of Jesus' day, many don't get that point, and we think that our sins are in check. We maintain that Sin is not an issue, that all is okay.

14 Now we know that the law is spiritual,
but I am of flesh,
sold into slavery under sin.
15 What I do, I do not understand.
Not what I want, that I do.
But what I hate, that I do.
16 Now if what I do not want, that I do,
I agree with the law that *it is* good.
17 So now *it is* no longer I doing it, but the sin dwelling within me.
18 For I know that good does not dwell within me, that is, in my flesh.
The willing *is* present with me, but doing the good *is* not.
19 For I do not do the good I want; but the evil I do not want, that I do.
20 Now if what I do not want, that I do,
it is no longer I doing it, but the sin dwelling within me.

21 So I find the law that when I want to do good, evil is present with me.

22 For I delight in God's law according to my inner self,

23 but I see another law in my members at war with the law of my mind,

and making me captive to the law of sin that dwells in my members.

24 Wretched one *that* I *am*! Who will rescue me from this body of death?

[Paul] 25 Thanks to God—through Jesus Anointed our Lord!

[Teacher of Law] So then, I myself, with the mind I serve God's law, but with the flesh, sin's law.

VV. 14–25

I agree with the law that it is good. As we are born we are not totally depraved; we still have a conscience that can perceive right and wrong. Where we are depraved is in our inability to do what we know to be right and our inability to resist that which we know to be wrong. There is a remnant of our original spirit that dwells in our soul: our conscience. It's as if we can tell what the spirit used to be by the shadow it casts on our actions. Is Sin a positive presence or a lack of Grace? It is both. Sin is an active and animate disposition that dwells in us by right. When we worship amiss, we invite the Devil into our hearts, and we become incapable of resisting his dictates. All, as we are born, are demon-possessed. We grow up worshipping as Adam did, for we are his spiritual heirs. However, when we, like the prodigal son, come to our right minds, we can exorcise ourselves by recognizing the Lordship of Jesus Christ. It's a zero-sum game with the Lord and the Devil: the more of one we have, the less of the other. We can't tell the Devil to go to hell, but we *can* ask Jesus to come in. This kind of invitation makes the Devil flee, for he cannot countenance the beauty, righteousness, or authority of the King of Kings. God only asks us to do what we can, not what we cannot. We can say, in effect, "Adam no longer speaks for me, and I give up the right to decide good and evil to the Lord and to his Word. My mouth is stopped." *Inner self, my inner being* (NIV) or *Law of my mind.* In spite of what Calvin says regarding total depravity, we can know right; we just can't do it.[5] We are corrupt, but not completely bereft. *In my mind, I myself am a slave to God's Law* (NIV). Our perception is undiminished; our response, however, is perverse.

5. "The Spirit is so contrasted with the flesh that no intermediate thing is left." Calvin, *Institutes*, 289.

Chapter 8

PRÉCIS

This chapter represents the end of the first overall C section, or conclusion, of this letter. As such, Paul dismisses the Law with its inherent shortcomings and embarks on a positive exposition of a better way: life in the Spirit. He bolsters his argument by introducing terminology derived from the human family; Christ makes it possible to join God's family. He then summarizes God's plan of redemption in the famous *Ordo Salutis*, the order of salvation.

[Paul] 8 Now then, *there is* no condemnation for those in Anointed Jesus.

2 For the law of the spirit of life in Anointed Jesus has freed you[34] from the law of sin and death.

3 For what the law could not do, in that it was weak through the flesh, God, sending his own son in likeness of flesh of sin, and for sin, condemned sin in the flesh,

4 so the requirement of the law may be fulfilled in us who walk not by flesh but by spirit.

5 For those who are by flesh mind the *things* of the flesh, but those by spirit the *things* of the spirit.

6 The mind of the flesh *is* death, the mind of the spirit *is* life and peace.

7 Because the mind of the flesh *is* hostility to God, to the law of God it does not submit, nor can it,

8 and those who are in flesh cannot please God. [ABBA] [End of dialogue that began at 7:7].

[34] 8:2 Here, *you* in Greek is singular in number. Paul is responding to the one who said *I* in 7:7–25.

V. 1

Now then or *therefore* (NIV). As we've seen before, modern chapter divisions serve to separate that which Paul meant to be a continuous thought. Verse 25 of the previous chapter should be connected to 8:1. There is a chiasmus in verses 2–6. The climax, the theme, is in verse 4, explaining the necessity of walking by the spirit and not the flesh. Earlier Paul has pointed out that redemption is a two-part process. Here he focuses on the second requirement, that Christ be *in us*. Again, Paul gives less emphasis to that which is automatic and universal, justification, and more to that which is particular and not automatic by any means, salvation. I will deal with this critical argument by pairing associated verses.

VV. 2, 6

Note how Paul expands the definition of law. Law is not just the Mosaic Law given on Mount Sinai, but it is now used to denote the creation principle that our spiritual decisions result in thoughts and behaviors that cannot be resisted. How we worship puts into motion a series of events that will rule us, for good or ill. We are free to decide on matters of worship, but having decided, we are no longer free. We must endure the consequences of our worship life, which work with the inviolability of a law. Here again is the idea of a zero-sum game. The more we have of one dominating influence, the less we have of the other. We cannot get rid of the law of sin and death, but we can focus on and subscribe to the law of the spirit of life in Jesus, and thereby we can push the other out. Paul continues the theme he introduced at the end of the previous chapter, that of God's merciful rescue. We issue the request; he provides the power. We have the power to decide which spiritual habitat we occupy. Our worship determines the identity of our Lord, and our Lord determines our spiritual destiny. Is our body in charge of our spirit, or is the Spirit in charge of our bodies? Behavior is subsequent to and determined by our intellectual allegiance, and that in turn is derivative of worship. Worship is depicted as a rudder that, though small in itself, can turn the ship to take advantage of the power of the wind. The mind, the intermediate agent, is also under the dominion of the Sin nature unless it is liberated through correct worship.

VV. 3, 5

Law here refers once again to the Mosaic Law. Earlier, in 5:9–10, Paul argues that we have two problems: guilt and powerlessness. We have sins that need forgiveness, but we also harbor Sin, a disposition of rebellion that galls Jesus, grieves his Holy Spirit, and makes it so that he is not in us effectually, though we are in him legally. God is not interested in just forgiving us, he wants to restore us to our former place in the Garden, where we did not live with a compulsion to sin. Here Paul argues that not only did the Cross cover sins, it also dealt with Sin as a ruling disposition. Those who are willing to crucify their own will and to be identified with Christ's death, will be able to harbor the Spirit with His life-giving power.

V. 4

Paul's conclusion is that the indwelling Spirit of Jesus can actually grant us power to do the things the Law of Moses commanded. We are not just reinstated to good standing, we are reconstituted to good disposition. God doesn't fix us; he replaces us. The solution to our powerlessness is to locate power from without and make it our own

VV. 7–8

We like to think we're rational: we take the facts, analyze them, deduce their implication, and conduct ourselves in keeping with what we know to be true. It is not so. Instead, we act according to our sinful and fleshly impulses, rationalize with our minds why it is okay, and then form our worship along those same lines. We're built upside down. Above all, the mind seeks to eliminate cognitive dissonance, so it becomes slave to the flesh. God, who wants us built right side up, is opposed to those who take their guidance from the flesh. God has decided, in *election* as properly understood, what kind of person is pleasing to him.[1] This is the person who is conformed to the essence and behavior God intended in creation. The person who continues to submit to the dictates of the flesh is abrogating the terms of God's plan of redemption, grieving the Holy Spirit, and thereby blaspheming him—the only unforgivable sin.[2]

United as God's sons and heirs in Anointed[35]

9 But you[36] are not in flesh but in spirit, if God's spirit dwells in you.
If anyone does not have Anointed's spirit, that one does not belong to him.

1. Exod 33:17–20.
2. Mark 3:29; Luke 12:10.

10 If Anointed *is* in you, the body *is* dead because of sin, but the spirit *is* life because of justfulness.

11 And if the spirit of him who raised Jesus from *the* dead dwells in you, he who raised Anointed from *the* dead, will give life also to your mortal bodies, through his spirit dwelling in you. [ABBA]

12 So then, brothers, we are debtors, not to the flesh, to live by flesh,

13 for if you live by flesh, you will die,

but if by spirit you put to death the deeds of the body, you will live.

14 For as many as by God's spirit are led, they are God's sons.

15 For you have not received a spirit of slavery back again into fear,

but you received a spirit of sons in which we cry, "Abba! Father!"

16 The spirit itself bears witness together with our spirit that we are God's children,

17 and if children, also heirs,

God's heirs,

and Anointed's fellow heirs,

if we suffer together so that we may also be glorified together.

[35] 8:9–39 ABCBA. 9–17 and 35–39, our relationship with God and the Anointed. 18–25, our hope. 26–30, God's help. 31–34, if God is for us who can be against us?

[36] 8:9 In verses 9–39, the Greek words for *you* are plural.

V. 9

If. There is no condition with justification, but there *is* a condition with salvation. Christ must be in us effectually, for it does us no good if we are only in him legally. God is interested in genuine restoration, not superficial technicalities. This mutual interpenetration between Christ and the believer is essential for full inclusion in the family of God. If Jesus, *Anointed*, is in us, the body is no longer capable of exercising control. The body is alive physically, but in spiritual terms it's no longer a danger because it's under control; it's not running amok.

V. 10

It's a willingness to accept vicarious justification and vicarious power that defines the person who is acceptable to God. It is a receptivity to the Spirit entering our hearts, the seat of our will, from without, that renders one elect. *Justfulness* or *righteousness* (NIV) comes from God and not from us, and it refers to the person who is both justified *and* living according to the Spirit.

V. 11

Essence determines destination. If Jesus was raised from the dead, though accounted guilty, so too, we who have him in us will be raised. The content of our spirit has an effect on our physical bodies as well. Just as Jesus was resurrected in body, so will our bodies be somehow preserved in vitality through the revolution in our spirits. This applies to this life, where our bodies cease to be a force of sin and rebellion, and to the life to come when we die.

VV. 12–17

What conclusion could we possibly come to other than we'd better live according to the spirit as opposed to the flesh? Who wants to die? There's supposed to be a death, but it's death to our will, not to our souls. Those who are obedient to the Spirit become in reality God's children and brothers to Jesus. Behavior counts, because it reveals what's in us spiritually. Instead of running from God in fear and nakedness, we are able to grasp his benevolence and realize he is our greatest advocate and benefactor, as a human father is to a young child.

Heirs. A child is both a biological heritor of their parent, and also a legal and fiduciary heritor. What is theirs becomes ours. *If we suffer.* Suffering was the lot of the Roman Christians under Nero. The good that Paul outlines may not be evident at present, but is real nonetheless. God rewards those who make right decisions, who undo the effects of Adam's sin by agreeing to no longer decide what's right and wrong for themselves, and who take God's word for what's good and bad. Paul always undergirds his pastoral admonitions to action by explaining the underlying spiritual dynamics.

> 18 For I consider that not comparable *are* the sufferings of this present time to the coming glory to be revealed for us.

V. 18

Paul is ever mindful that the saints in Rome are suffering. His pastoral side reemerges. He wants to explain how a loving God could delay the return of the Lord, his parousia, and thereby allow his saints to languish in persecution by the government, Jewish authorities, and pagans alike. A brief chiasmus tells us why.

> 19 For the anxious expectation of creation the revealing of God's sons awaits.
>
> 20 To futility
>
> creation was subjected,
>
> not of its own will
>
> but by him who subjected *it*,
>
> in hope
>
> 21 that creation itself will be freed from the slavery of corruption into the freedom of the glory of God's children.

VV. 19, 21

The purpose of the delay is to reveal the full number of God's children. There are still children of God who are in slavery to the law of sin and death, yet who will, with time, repent and be accounted God's children. It's the parable of the seeds and the tares all over again: to remove the bad would interfere with the growth of the righteous, so God delays.[3]

V. 20

The conclusion is that God is the author of the delay. By showing God to be slow to anger, he is revealed as loving and compassionate. The patience of the saints who suffer is therefore placed in the context of their contribution to the salvation of others who are still lost.

> 22 For we know that all creation together groans and suffers in labor pains until now.
>
> 23 And not only *creation*, but also ourselves, having the first fruit of the spirit,

3. Matt 13.

we also ourselves groan within ourselves, awaiting a status as sons,
the release of our body.
24 For in hope we were saved.
But hope seen is not hope.
For who hopes for what one sees?
25 But if we hope for what we do not see,
with patience we wait.

VV. 22–25

We are not the only ones suffering. The whole creation, made for our benefit, joins in the ordeal. We will not know our true identity as God's children until we die. Explaining the delay of the parousia and the death of saints in the meantime was one of the conundrums of the early church, and it was something that perplexed even Paul. To understand the present time and situation, we must consider the larger picture. Hope is the ability to focus on that which will happen in the future, in spite of the present reality. It is what sustains us as we wait.

26 In the same way, the spirit also comes to the aid of our weakness.
For what we should pray for as we ought we do not know,
but the spirit itself pleads with groans inexpressible.
27 And he who searches the hearts knows what *is* the mind of the spirit,
because according to *the will of* God it pleads for *the* holy *ones*.

VV. 26–27

It is not necessary that we understand what's going on; in many ways it makes no sense. But intellectual understanding is not what's important here. What is important is that we sense in our spirits that all this is for a purpose, that the lost be redeemed, and when frustrated, we can join with the Spirit in interceding for those who have yet to come to faith. Everything God does is for the purpose of redeeming his creation so that we might worship him properly.

28 And we know that, with those who love God,
all things he works for good,
with those who are called according to *his* purpose.

29 For those he knew before he also appointed before *to be* conformed to his son's likeness,

so that he may be the firstborn among many brothers.

30 And those he appointed[37] before he also called, and those he called he also justified, and those he justified he also glorified.

[37] 8:29,30 *Appointed*. Same word used in 1:4 for Jesus being "appointed God's son in power . . . by resurrection"

VV. 28–30

The famous *Ordo Salutis*, Order of Salvation, which has confounded many a Reformed theologian. I see a very important chiasmus in these verses that is not evident in Bailey's topology, but I insist. These three verses have led most commentators to assume that atonement is limited according to an arbitrary double predestination of individuals on God's part. Nothing could be farther from the truth. This eisegetical error is due to using syllogistic logic lifted from Aristotle and then implemented by Thomas Aquinas to convert a piece of Hebrew symmetrical parallelism into a linear sequence. Reading these three verses in a Greek or Western manner leads to the conclusion that foreknowledge precedes appointment, appointment precedes calling, calling precedes justification, and justification precedes glorification. It's easy to see why such an interpretation could portray God as justifying only those who have been selected by divine caprice. But note first of all that Paul joins these verbs together with the word, *also*, not *then*. The riddle is solved if you see it as a chiasmus. The events are additive or complimentary, not sequential or conditional. I will comment on the allied verses to better illustrate the chiastic structure.

Paul starts with a summary of the conclusion, C, in verse 28, the idea of calling, then explains who, exactly, is called. God calls those who love him, purely and simply. All that is happening to his Roman audience is good because God is allowing it. Suffering doesn't mean God has abandoned them, it actually means that God has chosen them and is going to redeem the present circumstances.

After stating his chosen subject, God's calling in difficult times, Paul puts that call in its proper context to show how following God is a blessing and not a curse. The argument he makes can be portrayed in the following manner:

A) 29 For those he knew before

B) he also appointed before *to be* conformed to his son's likeness, so that he may be the firstborn among many brothers. 30 And those he appointed before

C) he also called, and those he called

B) he also justified, and those he justified

A) he also glorified.

VV. 29A, 30D.

Those God foreknows he glorifies. Foreknowledge does not imply seeing what people would do in the future because God is outside of time, as Origen, Ambrose of Milan, Augustine, Arminius, and many others have suggested. Foreknowledge has to do with God's sovereign choice as to whom he will accept as his children. He has established a criterion of acceptability based upon his sovereign preference as head of the household. He is talking about a class or type of people, not individuals, as Arminius is helpful to point out.[4] He then glorifies those whom he has deemed to be his children. These are the monergistic decisions of God the *father*, as established in his eternal counsels, and they constitute the beginning and end of the chiasmus.

VV. 29B–30A, 30C.

Here we move to the actions of the *son*, Jesus the Anointed. These, too, are monergistic actions on God's part, but which involve Jesus and find manifestation in history. It is part of God's plan of redemption that people be fixed in reality as well as restored legally. Therefore, he *appoints* or *predestines* (NIV), that they be conformed to the likeness of Jesus and thereby bear a strong family resemblance to him.[5] Note that this term, *proorizō*, which Bailey translates as *appoints*, is used six times in the New Testament, and never refers to whether people go to heaven or hell, as is popularly believed. It always refers to something that is decided beforehand, but which finds its realization later on. That's all. The NIV also translates it as "decided beforehand" or "destined." It simply signifies that when it comes to God's plan of redemption, its rules and regulations are the result of divine decree and earthly events will reflect that decree. In this case, Paul is saying that when we make a right decision regarding worship, we get actual, tangible benefits

4. Arminius, "Analysis," 490.
5. Eph 1:5. " . . . adopted as his sons through Jesus Christ . . . ." (NIV)

in this life, each and every time. We become Christ-like. In this manner Jesus in us grants us power to live aright. This is the meaning of verse 29b. In 30b he mirrors this statement by saying that Jesus also justifies us in a forensic, legal sense, by dying on the Cross. We are justified by him, even if we worship amiss. In Jesus our primary problems are dealt with, both our powerlessness and our moral guilt. We experience sanctification first, in this life, but are assured that our sins are forgiven because of Christ's prior sacrifice as we approach death.

V. 30B

This is the conclusion, which should be read as a recapitulation of verse 28. This is the state Paul's readers find themselves in. They are *called* to their present state, a state in which they love God and endure trials. Jews are called through special revelation, Gentiles through general revelation. The call to each is refined and personalized when they submit to the Lordship of Jesus Christ. This is the life of the *Spirit*. Thus, we see a logical progression from the father's decision, to the son's contribution, to the current activity of the Spirit, and back to the son's action and the father's final action (AB-CBA.) A and B are monergistic, C is synergistic. This understanding allows us to reject the notion that justification is somehow late in the process and therefore limited in its extent. There is no limit to the atoning work of Christ on the Cross. The limitation occurs at the beginning of the process when God decides what kind of person, what class of people, he will accept into his family. This is the meaning of *choice*, *election*, or *foreknowledge*. God elects those who love him, who are willing to accept vicarious justification and empowerment, and he predestines them to sanctification and ultimate glory. He reprobates and rejects those who either deny their need of justification or empowerment, or who seek to achieve it by themselves apart from Christ. God resists those who seek to rob Christ of the glory that is due to him alone, and who willfully deviate from his perfect plan of redemption.

This is the *Ordo Salutis* from God's perspective. An accurate Ordo Salutis from a human point of view can be constructed from this chiasmus, along the following lines:

1. We hear the Gospel preached and our conscience bears witness to its truth. It emphasizes God's actions which brings assurance.
2. Such a gracious Savior has the right to be Lord; we cede our will to him.

3. The father confers the Holy Spirit on all that are disposed to receive both righteousness and power vicariously from Christ. Sanctification begins, and we are conformed more and more to the likeness of Christ.
4. Empowered by the Holy Spirit, we bear fruit in other lives.
5. At death, we receive glory and honor as a good and faithful servant.

31 What then shall we say to these? If God *is* for us, who *can be* against us?

32 He who "did not spare his own son" but handed him over for us all, how will he not also give us all things with him?

33 Who will bring a charge against God's chosen *ones*? "*It is* God who justifies.

34 Who will condemn?" *It is* Anointed who died, and more, was raised, who also is at God's right hand, who also intercedes for us.

35 Who will separate us from the Anointed's love?

Hardship, or distress, or persecution, or hunger, or nakedness, or
danger, or sword? 36 As it is written: "For your sake we are being
killed all the day long; we are counted as sheep for slaughter."

37 No, in all these things we are more than conquerors through him who loved us.

38 For I am convinced that neither death, nor life, nor angels, nor
rulers, nor things present, nor things to come, nor powers, 39 nor
height, nor depth, nor any other creature,

will be able to separate us from God's love in Anointed Jesus our Lord.

VV. 31–38

Paul returns to his pastoral concerns about the suffering the Roman congregation is enduring. He lists those things that are apparently the daily experience of the saints there: *hardship, distress, persecution, hunger, nakedness, danger*, and *sword*. These things, horrible as they are, can be put into context and endured, for though daunting, they are transitory and do not compare with the good that is just over the horizon. The spiritual domain, the fourth dimension, superintends and triumphs over that which is seen here and now. The first 17 verses of this chapter outline the process of sanctification, the difference Christ makes when he is *in us*. The remainder of the chapter explains how this knowledge allows us to have confidence in God and our fate in spite of our tribulations. As was outlined in chapter 5, endurance is to produce character.

Chapter 9

PRÉCIS

This chapter constitutes the start of the second C section of the letter, a conclusion that extends from 9:1 to 11:36. A suitable title for this section is "God's plan of redemption as experienced by Jew and Gentile." Paul has just been dealing with abstract theory, and now he backs up his arguments by citing his source of authority: Holy Scripture. His audience is the Jews, and he searches their Bible for examples that confirm in history what he's affirmed in theory. Ignoring Paul's dependence upon tools of Hebrew rhetoric, many commentators have misunderstood this chapter with grave consequences for Christian theology.

Israel and Gentiles are interdependent for salvation[38]

Doxology to the Israelites and blessing to God[39]

9 Truth I am telling, in Anointed, I am not lying, [ABA]
bearing witness to me *is* my conscience in holy spirit,
2 that sorrow to me is great and unceasing anguish in my heart.
3 For I have been praying to be **cursed**[40], myself, I, separated from the Anointed, [ABA]
for the sake of my brothers, my kinsmen according to flesh,
4 who are Israelites,
whose *are* the status of sons,
and the **glory**,
and the covenants,
and the law giving,
and the *temple* worship,

and the promises,
5 whose *are* the fathers,
and from whom *is* the Anointed according to flesh.
He who is over all, God,[41] **blessed** into the ages. Amen. [ABA]

[38] 9:1—11:36 ABCCBA. A's: doxologies, B's: God's purposes in saving part and hardening part of Israel, C's: why?

[39] 9:1–5 ABA. Parallel with 11:33–36. The first and last sections contrast Paul with God, but both are concerned for those at the center, the Israelites. Note the use of *glory* (*doxa* in Greek) in 9:4 and 11:36.

[40] 9:3 *Cursed*, as the Anointed became "for us" (Gal 3:13) and as Moses asked God to erase his name from the book of life if God would not forgive the people of Israel (Ex 32:32).

[41] 9:5 *God*. The word sequence in verse 5 follows the Greek exactly.

VV. 1–5

Paul's now talking to Jews again—not just the five or so in the Roman congregation, but rhetorically, to all Jews. He wants them to know that although he appears to be throwing them under the bus, he does so with heartfelt regret. Their error is due to defects in character, but this does not lessen the pain that he feels for his compatriots according to the flesh. He's been accused elsewhere of neglecting Jewish observances and devoting too much energy to minister to Gentile sinners, so he wants to emphasize the fact that in spite of mistakes, special revelation starts and ends with Jews. There's brief and irregular chiasmus here, as Paul lists the elements of special revelation that have been afforded the Jews. The associated elements will be paired.

VV. 4A–B, 4G–5A

Israelites are already counted as sons of God because they are sons of Jacob who became Israel. The family theme continues in 5a with the mention of *patriarchs* (NIV), literally *fathers*, and Jesus, the ultimate son of God. The idea is that God made them sons, sons by way of promise, but they can remove themselves from the family through willful effort. They are later importuned to *abide* where they have been placed, not to break out and depart like a prodigal son.[1]

1. Luke 15.

VV. 4C, F

God's glory was first witnessed as Moses led the Israelites in their flight from Egypt and their sojourn in the desert. It was also manifested at Mount Sinai, in God's passing by Moses, and is later associated with the tabernacle and the temple in Jerusalem. That glory is linked with temple worship in this litany.

VV. 4D–E

Logically the covenants and law-giving constitute the conclusion of Paul's case stating the privilege of special revelation. He will, however, make a distinction between the Abrahamic and Mosaic covenants as he goes on. The former abides, as it points beyond itself to its fulfillment in Christ. The Mosaic covenant given on Mount Sinai and the Law, however, are stopgap measures designed to bring about frustration and repentance, not success.

VV. 5B–C

People wonder if Paul attests to the divinity of Christ. Here it is.

A remnant will be called and saved from Israel, and also from Gentiles[42]

6 Not as though God's word has failed.
For not all those from Israel are Israel,
7 nor because they are Abraham's seed *are* all children,
but "In Isaac will seed be named to you."
8 That is, not the children of the flesh *are* these children of God,
but the children of the promise are counted as seed.
9 For this *is* the word of promise: "About this time I will return and
Sarah will have a son."

[42] 9:6–29 ABCCBA. Parallel with 11:11–32. 6–9 and 27–29, not all Israel are Israel. 10–13 and 22–26, some non-Israelites chosen and some not. 14–18 and 19–21, some chosen for mercy or honor and some not.

VV. 6A, 9

After the brief rapture about specific revelation, the theme of Israel's failure continues. How can it be that a holy God has a perfect plan of redemption for his sinful humanity, yet that plan appears to be ineffective? God gave his word, his promise, to Abraham, yet many of his children have rebelled against that plan. Paul launches into an explanation that has confused many a commentator, that confusion leading to most of the theological errors that plague the church today. Paul can be counted on to use his most effective rhetorical devices when making an important point, and as such, a brief chiasmus extends from verse 6 to 9. The apparent failure of a racial or biological covenant is contrasted with the word of promise that did in fact produce a son, Isaac. Sarah's son is uniquely a child of promise, conceived against all odds and in stark contrast to the inferior circumstances surrounding the birth of Ishmael. Like so many recurring words, *promise* is very specific in its meaning. Flesh stands for what we do; promise stands for what God does, his entire plan of redemption.

VV. 6B, 8B

Spiritual identity does not necessarily correspond with racial identity. This point is brought home by Jesus in his dealings with the centurion, the woman from Syrian Phoenicia, and the woman at the well at Sychar.[2] These foreigners proved themselves to be Jewish at heart if not in the flesh. Jewishness to Jesus was a reverence for the elements of specific revelation, especially the messianic hope of which he was the fulfillment. Thus, the Promise Paul refers to is the expectation that a Messiah will come and bring true spiritual liberty. Israel's children will be determined on the basis of their character, not their genes. This is the true meaning of *election*.

VV. 7A, 8A

The issue is family membership. Whereas earthly families, and the Jews up to this time, are established through the flesh, the heavenly family of God will be determined according to a new criterion. Here the old standard of carnal reproduction is dismissed.

V. 7B

This is the conclusion of the chiasmus. After the negation comes the positive assertion. To be accounted a child of God in the new economy, one must be descended from Isaac. His birth is juxtaposed with that of Ishmael. Isaac is a child of promise, as per verse 9, while Ishmael is a child of the flesh. Ishmael

2. Matt 8:5–13; Mark 7:24–30; John 4:4–42.

here serves as a metaphor, and represents all who would seek to circumvent, emend, bypass, or simply help along God's promise through human ingenuity.[3] He is the poster child for all who take shortcuts, for those who use the intellect to subvert God's will in his plan of redemption. He represents a type or class of people who worship amiss by substituting their own plans for God's. As Paul has already pointed out in the previous chapter, the mind conceives sins when it is under the dominion of Sin. The sin was not Sarah's nor Hagar's alone, it was also Ishmael's. Ishmael, it is recorded, was *mocking* (NIV) or *at play* during the feast Abraham threw to celebrate Isaac's weaning.[4] He derogated Abraham's preference for Isaac and showed disrespect for his father. He worshipped amiss, and he tried to insinuate himself into a heritage by works, as would the Jews later on.

> 10 And not only *that*, but also Rebecca, having conceived by one, Isaac our father,
>
> 11 before they had been born or had done anything good or bad,
>
> so that according to choice God's purpose might stand—
>
> 12 not because of works but because of calling—
>
> she was told: "The older will serve the younger." 13 As it is written: "Jacob I loved, but Esau I hated."

VV. 10, 12B–13

This is another chiasmus. As with his father, Abraham, Isaac's genetic contribution is not sufficient to preclude reprobation in subsequent generations. Paul presses the point. Unlike Ishmael, who shared a father but not a mother with Isaac, Jacob and Esau had the same parents. Yet even in their case, one was counted for election and one for reprobation. Rebecca was told, in contrast to the established custom of primogeniture, that the older would serve the younger, for God loved Jacob but hated Esau. Note that God did not hate Esau for no reason. He hated him for a very specific reason: Esau represents all those who disobey God and his delegated authorities by favoring their physical needs over their spiritual obligations.[5] If Ishmael stood for those who follow intrigue instead of God's word, Esau is a metaphor for those who follow their bodies instead of that same word. This is a

3. See Gal 4:21–31. "These things may be taken figuratively . . . ."
4. Gen 16:1–2; Gen 21:9–10. See NIV Study Bible note for alternative translation.
5. Gen 25:29–34; Heb 12:16–17.

large class, or type, of humanity indeed. Esau speaks for many when he says, "Look, I am about to die."[6]

As it is written refers to Malachi 1:2b, 3a. This statement is made to refute Israel's claim that their misfortunes were due to God hating them. The Lord is saying, in effect, what if you want to see what it's like when God hates a nation, look no further than Edom. Again, Israel is still a land of promise and Edom a land of wrath; each is a manifestation of the spiritual heritage earned by their progenitors.

VV. 11–12A

Before . . . they had done anything good or bad. This appears to be an argument that election is based upon arbitrary choice, and not the merits or demerits of individuals or classes of people. After all, Jacob and Esau's fates were decided before they were born. I would argue, however, that this is really saying that God's election of *any* who please him and the rejection or reprobation of *any* who displease him were already decided before *any* was born. In other words, election as a divine decree precedes human activity, but it does not determine it. God did not ordain that Esau should despise his birthright, but he did ordain that those who despise their birthright and favor their bodily demands over proper worship would be subject to reprobation. Esau acted out of free will, which in turn was determined by wrong worship. His spirit was bereft, his mind was deluded, and his body was in charge. He also serves as a type or metaphor for the Jews, who plead for a blessing of their own, knowing that God's blessing has already been given to another, a child of promise, Jesus. The explanation is forthcoming.

V. 11B

The conclusion of the chiasmus. Paul points out that *choice* or *election* (NIV) stands inviolate. He states that God calls all, and he elects not those who strive to please with works, but rather those who cling to the promise.[7]

> 14 What then should we say? Injustice with God? Not at all!
>
> 15 For to Moses he says: "I will show mercy on whom I show mercy, and I will have compassion on whom I have compassion."
>
> 16 So then *it is* not of willing nor of working, but of God showing mercy.

6. Gen 25:32.
7. Arminius, "Analysis," 493–94.

17 For the scripture says to Pharaoh: "I have raised you up for this purpose, so I may show my power in you, and so my name may be proclaimed in all the earth."

18 So then he has mercy on whom he wills, and he hardens whom he wills.

VV. 14–18

The natural tendency of man, who always seeks to justify himself, is to say that it is unjust of God to have an absolute standard of judgment. Paul points out that God is entitled to this right. The quote from Moses was taken from an exchange between God and him in which Moses asks God to stay with Israel to show his pleasure in them. God acquiesces, saying that he is indeed pleased with Moses whom he knows by name.[8] The text in Exodus Paul chooses could not be more clear: God's choice is anything but arbitrary. Rather it is based upon the behavior of his children. The Old Testament references militate against the interpretations usually proffered by those in the Reformed tradition.

For God to call his children is the supreme form of mercy. By *willing* or *man's desire* (NIV), we understand the sexual drive to reproduce according to the flesh or race, and by *working* or *effort* (NIV), we understand works righteousness. The Jews relied upon both, yet neither worked. Those who try to please God by race or works are robbing God and Christ of the glory that is due them alone.[9]

Paul uses a third example of wrong worship and consequent wrong behavior that God has chosen to censure, thus constituting grounds for reprobation. Pharaoh thought himself the deputy of the sun god, Ra,[10] the intermediary between god and man. He states, "Who is the Lord that I should obey him?"[11] As such, he represents those who worship amiss in the spiritual realm, calling on gods who would compete with the Lord. Pharaoh was raised up for the purpose of showing what happens when we worship self or false gods. We will all glorify God somehow, either by our salvation or our destruction.

At this time, it is important to summarize the doctrine revealed in verses 6–18. Man has three constituent features: he consists of a soul, which is his mind, will, and emotions; a body; and a spirit. The latter is implied

8. Exod 33:17–20.

9. Luther, *Commentary*, 19.

10. Perhaps Thutmose II (1493–2 to 1479 BC.)

11. Exod 5:2.

when it says we were created in God's image.[12] Each of these component parts constitutes an avenue of attack for the Enemy who wishes to derail our spiritual progress. Paul chooses his examples from sacred history carefully, to reflect this three-pronged strategy. Ishmael represents those who use the mind to "assist" God through short cuts, Esau represents those who ignore God on account of physical appetites, and Pharaoh represents those who replace God with other spiritual entities capable of commanding worship. In addition to recounting the experiences of these individuals, Paul offers each as a metaphor for a type or class of person who succumbs to a temptation that is proscribed by God. In his eternal counsels, God has decided that each of these three tactics constitutes an evasion and perversion of his perfect plan of redemption and renders the practitioner subject to reprobation. In each case, the spiritual error precedes reprobation in chronological time. Individuals are not reprobate until they place themselves in one of these camps through deliberate choice.

Paul now juxtaposes mercy with hardening. *Hardens* is another word with a very specific meaning for Paul. He's referring to a phenomenon he outlined in chapter 1, where it is described as a step in the process whereby God's wrath is made manifest in the lives of men while they yet live. Note the present, continuous tense.[13] The process is set in motion when men fail to glorify God or give him thanks. God's response is to frustrate their thinking and darken their hearts. I would argue this darkening is synonymous with hardening. The final result of wrong worship is degrading behavior, particularly sexual perversions. Why does God harden? He does so for two reasons. First of all, in his infinite love and mercy, God desires the repentance of all and the death of none, so hardening is a last-ditch effort to help a man come to his senses.[14] All stand justified as a result of Christ's death, and to a certain extent all people, thus cleansed, are given a conscience that leads them to God and his divine will. When God wishes to show us what life, and indeed eternity, are like apart from himself, he withdraws whatever measure of grace we are granted by nature,[15] and we are left entirely to our own devices.[16] The resulting degradation and misery are intended to bring us to our right minds that we might repent and chart a new course.[17] God

12. Gen 1:27.

13. Rom 1:18.

14. Luke 15:17.

15. Rom 2:15, which probably refers to Gentiles after spirit baptism. See also John 15:5.

16. Matt 25:29; Luke 19:26b.

17. Note the case of AIDS. AIDS is not a disease, but rather the absence of an immune system designed to protect us from the assault of disease. When people persist

always favors the long term over the short, the spiritual over the physical, and reality over appearance.

The second reason God hardens those who persist in sin is to make them an example to other sinners and to show those already converted that he is indeed a patient and merciful father. He doesn't immediately kill those who defame him. He organizes creation to reward the good and punish the wicked. Seeing the rational basis of creation, sinners will conclude that God, too, is rational.

19 You will say to me then, "Why does he still find fault?
For who has withstood his will?"
20 O mortal, indeed, who are you to talk back to God?
"Will the molded say to the molder, Why did you make me like this?"
21 Has not the potter authority over the clay,
out of the same lump to make one vessel for honor and another for dishonor?

VV. 19–21

Paul uses the analogy of a potter with a piece of clay to show how God, even as we live, is turning us in a manner to bring out the best in us. The objection is to having been hardened. God made us like this, hardened us, because we provoked him to do so, and he does it with the intention of bringing us to repentance. Hardness is no fun, nor is it supposed to be. We ultimately determine what kind of vessel we become, and the trials and difficulties of life are designed to make us choose aright. It is only the dull and obdurate who charge God with injustice when things don't go according to plan. A hard heart leads to dishonorable behavior each and every time. It doesn't have to be the last word, but if we don't reconsider our worship life, our dishonor will be eternal.

22 What if God, desiring to show vengeance and to make known his power,
has endured with much patience *the* vessels of vengeance designed for destruction,

---

in sexual sins and refuse to listen to God, he may withdraw his protection—in this case the immune system—to show what life is like on one's own in a biological sense. People seek freedom but get solitude. I have personally led a homosexual man to faith in Christ because he was dying of AIDS and was thus forced to rethink his independence from God.

23 that he may make known the riches of his glory for vessels of mercy, which he has prepared beforehand for glory,

VV. 22–23

Vengeance again, or *wrath*. Calvin is correct when he contrasts the fate of the objects of God's wrath and the objects of his mercy.[18] The one puts the other in its proper light. The intended audience for this display of patience are the objects of his mercy. We are to see in his self-restraint the depths of his love and willingness to tolerate abuse in the hopes that time and circumstances will change hearts and people will repent.[19] The objects of his wrath were not prepared for the express purpose of destruction, as Calvin attests, but destruction was ordained for such as these in God's eternal counsels. The decision that this type of behavior should result in reprobation was eternal, but the actual failure of members of this class was left to time in human history.

Wrath is not just a decision on God's part having to do with a future judgment, but it is also manifest in this life.[20] The temporal wrath of God is manifested by the hardening already addressed. As such it occurs so that the fruit of wrong worship will be manifest to all, both good and bad. Wrath is displayed now so as to scare the sinner and help him come to his right mind.[21] It is also to lead the regenerate to worship, as God is preserving his creation that they might benefit.[22]

24 even us whom he has called, not only from Jews but also from Gentiles?

25 As indeed he says in Hosea: "I will call those not my people, 'my people,'

and her who was not beloved, 'beloved.'"

26 "And it will be in the place where it was said to them, 'You *are* not my people,' there they will be called 'sons of *the* living God.'"

27 And Isaiah cries out concerning Israel: "Though the number of the Israelites be as the sand of the sea, *only* the remnant will be saved,

18. "A second answer, by which he briefly shows, that though the counsel of God is in fact incomprehensible, yet his unblameable justice shines forth no less in the perdition of the reprobate than in the salvation of the elect." Calvin, *Commentaries*, 366.

19. 1 Tim 2:4.

20. Rom 1:18.

21. Heb 12:5–11.

22. Matt 13:29–30.

28 for *his* word, decisively and swiftly, *the* Lord will execute on the earth."

29 And as Isaiah foretold: "If *the* Lord of hosts had not left us a seed, like Sodom we would have been and like Gomorrah we would have been made."

VV. 24–29

Paul never misses an opportunity to emphasize his underlying argument, that Jews and Gentiles are on an equal footing in God's plan of redemption. He doesn't prepare *individuals* for glory—the preparation was that an entire class of people should be ordained to glory. The calling of individuals is the result of the election of types. They are two sides of the same coin. Paul goes back to the Jewish Bible to buttress his point, back to the very document Jews rely upon to show their spiritual preeminence. The quotes from Hosea chapters 1 and 2 and Isaiah show that the unfaithfulness of the Jewish nation would result in the expansion of the Gospel to the Gentile world.

Gentiles found what they did not seek, Israel has not found what it sought[43]

30 What then should we say?

That Gentiles, who did not pursue justfulness, have overtaken justfulness,

the justfulness from faithfulness,

31 but Israel who pursued, a law, of justfulness, to *that* law, has not attained. [ABCBA]

32 Why?

Because not through faithfulness, but as through works.

They have stumbled over the stumbling stone,

33 as it is written: "See, I lay in Zion a stumbling stone and a tripping rock,

and one who has faith in him will not be put to shame."

[43] 9:30—10:21 ABBA. Parallel with 11:1–10. A's, Israel pursuing, not finding; B's, salvation open to all.

VV. 30–33

What counts in obtaining righteousness is not the fervency of those seeking it, but rather the rectitude of the basis upon which they seek it. God gives righteousness, *ascribes* it, to all people freely, both Jew and Gentile, but he does so on a very specific basis. To go outside that basis is to criticize God as the One who decreed it, and to try to beat down the door to heaven by another route. Faith is a willingness to accept both justification and salvation on a vicarious basis, without reference to one's own efforts or merits. The Jews were largely unwilling to accept this secondary role and strove to keep themselves as primary agents in generating righteousness.

Elsewhere Jesus has been referred to as a rock,[23] the image being one of substance and weight. Because the Jews were unwilling to give Jesus thanks and glory for his role in their redemption, they failed in their spiritual destiny. Christ is central to God's plan of redemption, and to try to remove that which is integral to a logical plan will result in failure. Both pagan license and Jewish religion rob Christ of his glory. In a related metaphor, Jesus himself says that he is a stone, and active resistance as well as passive indifference result in disaster.[24]

23. Exod 17:6; Deut 32; 1 Cor 10:4; 1 Pet 2:4–8.

24. Luke 20:18.

Chapter 10

PRÉCIS

God redeems humanity freely, but he does so on a very specific basis. Those who stray from God's plan of redemption exclude themselves from the benefits of that plan. Salvation is not automatic; it requires a response from us that is volitional. Paul lays out what that response must be, pointing out that it has two dimensions. There is an acceptance of Christ as Savior, and a subsequent submission to that same Christ as Lord. Paul defines the concept of a call, when all that God has done for his larger creation becomes intensely personal.

> **10** Brothers, my heart's desire and prayer to God for them *is* for salvation.
>
> 2 I bear them witness that they have zeal for God, but not according to knowledge.

VV. 1–2

Paul reiterates his desire that the Jewish nation be successfully redeemed. Note his precision. He does not say he wants the Jews justified; he speaks of their salvation, which is the second half of the equation of redemption. Justification is assured; it's salvation that is optional and depends on the response of the individual. Success in responding to God does not depend upon zeal or earnestness, but upon conformance to the plan He has already put in place. Their problem, as stated before, is that they wanted to generate a *righteousness* (NIV), a *justfulness*, of their own and not accept vicarious righteousness from God.

3 Not knowing, God's, justfulness, and their own, seeking to establish, [ABCBA]
to the justfulness of God they did not submit.
4 For *the* fulfillment[44] of *the* law *is* Anointed,
for justfulness to everyone who is faithful.
5 Moses describes the justfulness that *comes* from law,
"the one who does these will live in them."

[44] 10:4 *Fulfillment*? *Goal*? Or *end*? See 3:31; 7:12,14a; 8:2–4; 13:8–10. This verse may explain 3:19 and 11:32.

VV. 3A, 5

Bailey sees a chiasmus in verses 3–5 wherein Paul describes the error of the Jews contrasted with the success of the Anointed. Not wanting to humble themselves by accepting God's righteousness, they seek to establish their own in verse 3, which corresponds with legal performance in verse 5. They think that by obeying the Law they will find life.

VV. 3B, 4B

This is the basis upon which God's righteousness is offered. It can be rejected through personal willfulness, but it is not withheld arbitrarily by God. It requires submission. We have to cede our will and our pride to God before we can benefit from the righteousness that is by faith as opposed to works.

V. 4A

The conclusion: only Christ can fulfill the law and thereby justify humanity. Without him there is no justification, no redemption.

6 But the justfulness from faithfulness speaks in this way:
"Do not say in your heart,
'Who will go up into heaven?'
(that is, Anointed to bring down)
7 or 'Who will go down into the abyss?'

(that is, Anointed from *the* dead to bring up)."
8 But what does it say? "The word is near you, in your mouth and in your heart"
(that is, the word of faithfulness which we preach).

VV. 6A–B, 8

This is another rhetorical structure. *Justfulness from faithfulness* or *righteousness that is by faith* (NIV) speaks; it has a living essence, a reality that demands expression and reception. It involves both negative rejection and positive affirmation. In other words, it's possible to get this wrong, to grieve and abrogate the process, just as it's possible to grieve and reject a person. There is propositional content, truth, to the word being spoken. We've been given a brain, and we're expected to use it. Our heart is capable of decision, and our mouth is capable of enunciation. They are the seat of volition and the organ of expression. With the one, we believe—or, a better interpretation would be *resolve to obey*—and with the other, we *express* that which is already decided in the inner man. Notice what Paul means by preaching. He doesn't mean talking to no end. He means presenting a logical, consistent, fact-filled challenge to the mind and heart.

VV. 6C–D, 7

Paul says in Romans 1:21 that the proper response to God is to glorify him and give him thanks. We give him thanks because he sent his son to die for us on the Cross, to justify us. We glorify him because his son reigns as a living Lord who merits our unqualified worship and obedience. There are two facts regarding what God has done for us in Christ, and there are two occasions for us to offer worship. By way of contrast, here are two opportunities to make mistakes and get into spiritual trouble: the first error we can commit is to deny our guilt, to say that we don't need a Savior and can achieve righteousness on our own. This would be to try to *go up into heaven* on our own merits, the classic error of the Jew. By attempting this we are robbing Christ of his glory as the Son of Man. The second error we can commit is to deny our powerlessness and try to reform ourselves on an ongoing basis. To do this is to say that we don't need the infusion of power from a living Lord á la Pelagius. This is to say that Christ died, remains in the grave, and we have no need of a Lord. Note the Roman church always has a dead Jesus on their crucifixes. They focus on his substitutionary atonement, while forgetting that he rose and reigns as Lord. By saying he's in *the abyss*, we're denying his ongoing role as Son of God who left the abyss after three days. He's not only our Savior, he's also our Lord. In this regard, many Christians are preaching half the Gospel—the first half or the second half—but rarely both. Half the Gospel, it turns out, is no Gospel at all. The Gospel consists of two halves. Paul never tires of telling us of both, and people never tire of denying one or the other.

> 9 For if you confess with your mouth *the* Lord Jesus,
> and believe in your heart that God raised him from *the* dead,
> you will be saved.
> 10 For with *the* heart one believes to justfulness,
> and with *the* mouth one confesses to salvation.

VV. 9A, 10B

Here is another brief but critical chiasmus, taking the form ABCBA. This is an echo of 5:9–10, and Paul reiterates the distinction between justification and salvation. He starts and ends with a discussion of the role the mouth plays in the redemption of an individual. The mouth is the organ of expression for the human heart, and here it represents our response to what God has done. He is indeed looking for a response from us, and here it is. What we're supposed to say is that Jesus is Lord, his second title. When we make Jesus our Lord, by doing what he says and not doing what he proscribes, then we bear fruit and are accorded salvation. Paul emphasizes that which is under *our* control; he starts and ends with it.

VV. 9B–10A

No longer the mouth, now the heart is the subject. The focus is not on what we do, but what God has done for us. We *believe*. Belief to a Jew cannot be separated from the will. If we believe something, it will change our behavior. Belief has nothing to do with intellectual assent but is about conversion of the heart. When we really believe that God raised Jesus from the dead, we are accepting a whole string of events. The resurrection of Jesus is proof that all that took place in Holy Week was an intentional and unbridled success. He was killed for our sins and raised for our justification.[1] His rising validated his sacrifice, and it is proof that he was adjudged righteous, which

1. Rom 4:25.

means that we can be too. This thought occurs in the interior of the chiasmus as it's a given and not open to human contravention.

V. 9C

This is the conclusion of the chiasmus. *Will* indicates something in the future for each of us, not something that is foreordained, but an option. Note the word is *saved*, not *justified*. Paul's terminology is consistent and precise.

> 11 For the scripture says, "Whoever has faith in him will not be put to shame."
>
> 12 For there is no distinction between Jew and Greek,
>
> since the same *is* Lord of all,
>
> being generous to all who call upon him.
>
> 13 For "whoever calls on the Lord's name will be saved."

VV. 11, 13

Paul can't help himself, and here he presents another rhetorical argument. *Whoever* or *anyone* (NIV) is used to encompass Jew and Gentile; God has no favorites. To be put to shame is to miss out on salvation. As Oswald Chambers says, "We will all feel very much ashamed if we do not yield to Jesus the areas of our lives He has asked us to yield to him."[2] To call upon the Lord equates with yielding our will to him. Note the Semitic link between calling with the mouth and yielding with our hearts. The two cannot be separated.

VV. 12A, C

This one verse has three sections, and traditional versification is not always worthwhile. *No distinction* is echoed by the word *all*; God's generosity is open to all.

V. 12B

This phrase is the conclusion of the argument. Because Jesus is, *in potential*, Lord of all, all can be saved. It comes down to Jesus and what he does as

2. Chambers, *My Utmost*, January 1.

Lord, not to our past. The Gospel demands we drop all that is past and look instead to the future. All liberation movements that are based upon the past, whether racial, personal, economic or political, are doomed to enervate the individual and rob Christ of his glory.

14 **How** then are they to call on whom they have not believed?

And **how** are they to believe of whom they have not heard?

And **how** are they to hear without preaching?

15 And **how** are they to preach unless they are sent?

As it is written: "**How** beautiful the feet of those who bring good news!"

16 But not all have obeyed the good news.

For Isaiah says, "Lord, who has believed what *they* heard from us?"

17 So faithfulness *comes* from hearing, and hearing through *the* word of Anointed.

18 But I ask, have they not heard? Yes, indeed: "Their voice has gone out to all the earth, and their words to the ends of the world."

19 But I ask, did Israel not understand?

First Moses says, "I will make you jealous, of *those who are* not a people, with a people without understanding, I will make you angry." [ABBA]

20 Then Isaiah is bold and says, "I was found by those not seeking me; I appeared to those not asking for me."

21 But to Israel he says, "All day long I have held out my hands to a disobedient and contrary people."

VV. 14A, 19A

The first chiasmus begins and ends with a question. *Call.* Calling can refer to God's call to us, or our response to him. Here, as in verse 13, it refers to the latter: our granting God a sovereign preference in our decision making. It is a capitulation to an extrinsic authority when we come to believe in, or more properly obey, that higher authority. The implication is that we can't submit to an authority until we know it is greater than our own. Yet, incredibly, Israel has not done this. How could they not take proper action after God had authenticated his son as the Messiah? Was their unbelief and inaction due to some lack of understanding?

VV. 14B, 18

Now Paul appears to be engaging in syllogistic reasoning: how if A, not B; how if B, not C; etc. This is indeed linear thinking using causal deduction. Yet for each element of logical behavior expected in the first half of the chiasmus, there's a corresponding illogical reaction of Jews in the second half. Belief is expected when a case is made for a propositional truth, what we hear with our ears. Yet even though they hear, the Jews refuse to believe. There is nobody in all Israel who has not heard the claims of Christ, for as Paul puts it, this was not done in a corner.[3]

VV. 14C, 17

Preaching is simply this: an organized, systematic exposition of the claims of Christ within the context of God's larger plan of redemption. Good preaching always leads to the matter of the will, our will. God grants salvation to all those who hear of the contest of wills between our Creator and ourselves, and who cede to the Creator. Good preaching is all about Jesus, and in a very real way, it is the Word of Jesus. The Holy Spirit animates our words with his own suasion and brings about faith in the hearts of the hearers.

VV. 15A, 16B

All preachers are called by God to the task and sent forth into the fields. Paul claims such a commission, yet his experience has been fairly consistent rejection by Jews. This unbelief was predicted by Isaiah. Everything that happened to Jesus first, and then Paul, was foreseen by God.

VV. 15B–16A

This is the conclusion of the structure. Paul quotes from Isaiah 52:7 to show that a proper reaction to skilled, commissioned preachers is to view their approach with joy. Their message makes their ministry one of beauty. Yet in spite of the inherent beauty of this ministry, not all have obeyed the good news. Typically, people find disobedience a source of release, but Paul shows that the proper response to tremendous news is not one of throwing off restraint but of obedience. We don't believe in God, we obey God. To the Eastern mind, the two are synonymous.

3. Acts 26:26.

V. 19B–21

Paul quotes Deuteronomy 32:21, part of Moses' prophecy before his final blessing of the tribes of Israel and subsequent death. In spite of God's rescue of Israel and his nurturing of them, in their prosperity they forgot God and provoked his anger through wrong worship. As a result, he is going to shift his blessings from them to people who had no prior knowledge of him or claim on his goodness. The Gentiles will be included in what was originally a race-based covenant reserved for the biological sons of Abraham. This is done, in God's love, to provoke Jews to repentance. God's wrath manifests itself in this life as well, that amendment of life might take place before death's final separation. Anger can be useful when it leads to change. Like Moses, so it is with Isaiah. Paul quotes Isaiah 65:1 where the prophet points out that wrong worship on the part of Israel is what provokes God to shift his attention from Israel to the Gentiles. Israel's crime? They refused God's gesture of preference, that he revealed himself to them first, and instead disobeyed his commands and manifested obstinacy. God is looking for a response from us, and it's one of obedience and contrition.

Chapter 11

PRÉCIS

This last section of the second conclusion is about how we should experience redemption. Paul's address is initially to Jews, because he wants to destroy their trust in works righteousness once and for all. He emphasizes the concept of hardening to demonstrate God's opposition to anybody, Jew or Gentile, who defies his plan of redemption. Paul assures us that people are hardened not on an arbitrary basis, but in response to their wrong approach to religion. Gentiles are warned that failure on the part of Jews does not constitute a basis for pride. Eventually, all will be united under the Lordship of Jesus Christ. In this context, Paul is able to define election in a way that does no harm to God's reputation.

The chosen obtained what Israel was seeking, the rest were hardened

11 I ask then, has God rejected his people? Not at all!
I too am an Israelite,
of Abraham's seed,
Benjamin's tribe.
2 God has not rejected his people whom he foreknew.

Do you not know what the scripture says through Elijah,
how he pleads with God against Israel?
3 "Lord, your prophets they have killed,
your altars they have torn down,
and I alone am left, and they seek my life."
4 But what is God's reply to him?

"I have reserved for myself seven thousand men who have not bowed a knee to Baal."

5 So also at this time a remnant,
chosen by grace, remains.
6 But if by grace, then not of works, otherwise grace is no longer grace.
7 What then?
What Israel is seeking, it has not obtained.
The chosen obtained *it*,
but the rest were hardened,

8 as it is written: "God gave them a spirit of stupor,
eyes that see not and ears that hear not, to this very day."
9 And David says: "Let their table become a snare and a trap and a stumbling block and a retribution for them,
10 let their eyes be darkened so they cannot see,
and their backs be bent always."

VV. 1A, 2A

From the last verse of the preceding chapter one could easily conclude that God has completely and finally rejected his people. Paul poses the obvious question: Is this so? God has indeed accepted Jews, but only those he foreknew. That is, he accepts those who live up to the standard he envisioned from before time and eternity as pleasing him, Jew as well as Gentile.

VV. 1B–D

Paul refers to himself as exhibit A that God's rejection of Jews is not complete. He is himself a Jew through and through, with pedigree.

VV. 2B–4

Paul cites Scripture to prove his point. Elijah jumbles all Israel together in his complaint to God about how they kill prophets and tear God's altars down. Elijah is himself on the run and offers himself as a case study. Yet God says what Paul has already pointed out, which is that there is a remnant who still please him because they have not fallen into wrong worship. God reserves unto felicity those who worship aright. He foreknew them in the abstract. This is the meaning of *election*.

VV. 5, 6

Paul is walking a knife edge, and he knows it. The criticism of his soteriology is that we somehow participate in our own redemption, through our own strength. He wants to preserve the notion that God's choice of certain people over others is not arbitrary, but at the same time it's not a work. Since the coming of Christ, the decision of God abides, and he continues to accept those who please him on account of their worship. Grace, again, is not some vague force, but rather the reality of Jesus dwelling in those who worship and obey him. It's Jesus doing the work in us, not we ourselves. Just as we must accept a vicarious sacrifice for our sins, we must accept a vicarious power in us to live aright. Grace dissolves when we try to do things under our own steam; the Holy Spirit brooks no competition.

V. 7

So much for the faithful remnant, what of the rest of Israel? They have fallen into the downward spiral of spiritual degeneration outlined in previous chapters. By attempting to please God with works as opposed to worship, Israel has not only ceded its place of privilege to Gentiles but has also herself become hardened. In his love, God has made their mental futility reflect their spiritual degeneration. There is always correspondence between the two, so that errors in the spiritual arena might be perceived and sensed in the intellectual. We are to perceive, here and now, the fruit of our worship, whether it is good or bad.

V. 8–10

Paul uses their own Scriptures to make his point, quoting both Deuteronomy 29:4 and Isaiah 29:10 to describe the process of hardening caused by wrong worship. It resembles sleep, in that the senses are deadened, and the faculties of perception become useless. When the spiritual will is not there, physical sensations cannot be processed. He also quotes Psalm 69:22–23, the context of which is a prophecy about the sufferings of Christ on the Cross, to the same end. Those who despise Jesus will suffer in both this life and the life to come. *Their table* refers to both their domestic life and their sustenance.

Part of Israel is hardened so both Gentiles and Israel may be saved[45]

11 I ask then, have they stumbled so as to fall? Not at all!

But by their misstep salvation *has come* to the Gentiles so as to make them jealous.

12 Now if their misstep *means* riches for *the* world,

and their falling short *of winning the race means* riches for *the* Gentiles,

how much more their completion *of the race will mean*![46]

13 To you, I am speaking, to the Gentiles.

Inasmuch then as I am an apostle to *the* Gentiles, my ministry I glorify,

14 that somehow I may make jealous *those of* my flesh, and save some of them.

15 For if their loss[47] *means the* reconciliation of *the* world,

what *will their* recovery *mean* if not life from *the* dead?

16 If the first fruit *is* holy, also the *whole* lump; and if the root *is* holy, also the branches.

17 But if some of the branches were broken off,

and you, being a wild olive shoot, were grafted in among them

and a sharer of the root of the richness of the olive tree you became,

18 do not boast over the branches.

If you do boast,

not you, the root, support, but the root, you. [ABCBA]

19 You will say then, "Branches were broken off

so I may be grafted in."

20 True. Because of unfaithfulness they were broken off;

but you stand because of faithfulness.

Do not be proud, but fear.

21 For if God did not spare the natural branches, neither will he spare you.

22 See then *the* kindness

and severity
of God:
to those who fell, severity,
but to you, God's kindness, if you continue in *his* kindness,
otherwise you too will be cut off.
23 And they also, if they do not continue in unfaithfulness, will be grafted in,
for God is able to graft them in again.
24 For if you have been cut from what is by nature a wild olive tree,
and grafted, contrary to nature, into a cultivated olive tree,
how much more these natural *branches* will be grafted into their own olive tree.

[45] 11:11–32 ABCBA. A's: disobedience of Israel has benefited Gentiles. B's: salvation of Gentiles will benefit Israel. The center, 11:16–24, an address to a wild olive shoot, where *you* is singular, warns that grace requires a fitting response.

[46] 11:11–12 Paul uses foot race terms here that echo the story of the foot race in the Funeral Games described in the *Iliad*, book 23, lines 740–792. The goddess Athena trips Ajax, who is in the lead, to favor Odysseus, who won first prize. Ajax stumbles but recovers to receive the handsome second prize. Here God has delayed the Jews so the Gentiles have time to benefit from the Anointed's faithfulness before the Jews recover when the Anointed returns (11:25–26).

[47] 11:15 *Loss*. The only other place this word is used in the NT is in Acts 27:22 where it is usually translated "loss" (no loss of life). If it is translated here as "rejection," as it usually is, this verse would be the only place in the Bible where it says that God has rejected his people Israel, and it would contradict 11:1–2. This verse is a restatement of 11:11–12.

V. 11

Paul now departs from his argument about the past history of Israel vis à vis God's plan of redemption, and starts to speculate, predict, about what the future holds. His basic premise is that past failings do not preclude future reformation. *They* refers to all of Israel to a man. *To fall* is to be irrevocably excluded from the new covenant of God's grace. His answer is no, not all and not forever. A *misstep* is an error, to be sure, but one quickly remedied. Paul, the psychologist, points out that jealousy is a strong motivator. God's blessings, once reserved to the Jews, are now being distributed to the Gentiles. The image of the jealous older brother from Luke 15 comes to mind.

V. 12

Paul equates the world and Gentiles. For the Jew, this is true. *Hā' gôyim*. There is the Jew, and then there is everybody else lumped together. *Misstep* is equated with falling short of winning a race. The NIV reads *fullness* while Bailey's translation reads *completion of the race*. The image is that Israel's disobedience and reliance upon works is a predicted yet temporary setback that will one day be remedied.

VV. 13–14

Paul formally addresses the Gentiles, who have to this point been hearing plenty about the shortcomings of the Jews. Paul points out that the Jews are something of an example of normal human nature, and if it can happen to them, it can happen to anybody. Paul's not above bragging about his success with the Gentiles in order to provoke jealousy on the part of Jews. Jews must register some sort of interest if they are to be saved, because God demands a response from them.

V. 15

While the NIV reads *rejection*, Bailey's translation reads *loss*. Bailey argues that the former would suggest that God has finally and completely rejected Israel, which would contradict the entire argument Paul is making here. Further, loss is in keeping with its use in 1 Corinthians 6:7, which the NIV renders as *defeated*. We also read *recovery* as opposed to the NIV's *acceptance*. This places the agency for their reinstatement in their own hands as opposed to God's. *Life from the dead*. Right worship is the *sine qua non* of existence. If we get worship wrong, all is lost, and death prevails. Get it right, and life breaks forth.

VV. 16–17

Holiness requires drawing upon an outside source, God. He has been revealing himself for generations, and all of that revelation is valid as far as it goes. Just because that revelation has found its completion in Christ, that which came before is not invalid, it is still edifying. The first fruit in this case is the specific revelation accorded to Israel. The Gentiles have come later, and their holiness depends upon the groundwork already laid for the

Jews. Paul uses the analogy of an olive tree, well known to his audience and the object of selective breeding and grafting, to show that Gentiles are dependent upon the heritage of the Jews. Sequence implies priority, and lower priority should result in humility.

VV. 18–21

Paul warns against boasting directed against Jews, and then he says why. First of all, there's the idea that the Gentiles owe a debt to the Jews, for the Jews have kept the revelation of God alive and played host to Jesus, their Messiah. They have preserved the Scriptures which contain the Law and Prophets, which direct the reader to know God's will for his creatures. Verse 18c is a mini chiasmus. It starts and ends with *you*; proceeds to focus on the source of power, the *root*; and concludes with the active concept, *support*. Secondly, don't boast because the same fate awaits the Gentile who gets it wrong as the Jew who's already gotten it wrong. Just as with calling, there's no favoritism with reprobation.

VV. 22–24

God adjusts his response to his children based upon their behavior. He's kind to those who worship, and therefore behave, aright, but he's rough on those who don't. And he's not just interested in how we start, he cares about how we continue. It's a race, to use Paul's words, and probably not a sprint. What counts is not where we are in absolute terms so much as the direction in which we're headed. We can start out right and get it wrong; we can also start out wrong and then get it right. The latter is the prophecy Paul makes about the Jews. *Do not continue in unfaithfulness* is a double negative, and it can be understood to mean "start being faithful." The reintegration of Israel into the church will actually be easier than the in-grafting of the Gentiles, for Jews already possess the culture of proper worship. Jews don't need to be told that there's only one God, that he reveals himself to his people through the spoken and written Word, and that he cares about moral behavior and calls his people to personal holiness. Apart from Christ, a Jew is better off than a pagan, and maintains his head start when they both meet Christ, theoretically.

> 25 I do not want you to be unaware, brothers, of this mystery,[48] so you do not become conceited:

that a hardening has come upon part of Israel until the fullness of the Gentiles has come in.

26 And in this way all Israel will be saved, as it is written:

"The savior will come from Zion, he will turn away godlessness from Jacob."

27 "And this *is* my covenant with them, when I take away their sins."

28 As regards the good news, *they are* enemies for your sake,
but as regards the choosing, *they are* loved for the sake of the fathers.

29 For irrevocable *are* the gifts and the call of God.
30 Just as you *Gentiles* once disobeyed God,
but now you have received mercy
because of their disobedience,
31 so also they have now disobeyed
because of the mercy shown to you,
so that they too may receive mercy.
32 For God has imprisoned all in disobedience,
so that to all he may show mercy.[49]

[48] 11:25 The *mystery* described in 11:11–12,15,25–36 is that a temporary hardening has come upon part of Israel to give an opportunity for the Gentiles to be saved through the resurrection of the Anointed. Ultimately all Israel will be saved when the Anointed returns (11:26) (See 2 Pet 3:15–16). In 16:25 the mystery may refer to the division of God's prophesied Parousia (presence, coming) into two stages: the first stage being the resurrection of Jesus Anointed (1:4), which delayed the final judgment and gave Gentiles (16:26) an opportunity to share in that resurrection; and the second stage being the Anointed's return mentioned in 2:5,16; 8:18–25; 11:26; and 13:11–12, which Paul expected imminently. In 16:25 the focus is on its effect on the Gentiles—that God has included the Gentiles in his gifts of status as sons and the opportunity to respond with faithfulness. The mystery in 11:25–36 looks at the same division of God's parousia into two stages and its resulting delay, but from the point of view of its effect on the Jews: that they have been temporarily hardened during the interval between the two stages. Another extensive, and much simpler, explanation of the mystery of the inclusion of the Gentiles is in Eph 2:11–3:13. See "mystery" in the introduction to Colossians.

[49] 11:32 This verse restates the argument in 3:19–22 and 10:4.

V. 25

Mystery is not something that can't be known. Rather, it's a very specific event that's mysterious not because it's vague, but because it's unimaginable.

How can it be that Jew and Gentile—separated by all of specific revelation and ensuing history, by blood and temperament, religion and philosophy—might be reunited in one fell swoop by God's sovereign decree? God has ordained a hardening, which is for the benefit of those with no prior claim to God. This hardening has only come on part of Israel, not the whole nation. In addition to being limited in scope, it's also limited in duration; *until the fullness of the Gentiles has come in*. The NIV reads *full number*. I prefer Bailey's translation, as we're not talking about reaching some specific number of individuals. Rather, this encompassed the full range of non-Jewish peoples, the rest of the world: *hā'* gôyim. There is no people group, culture, or religion beyond the scope of God's new inclusivity.

VV. 26–31

Paul predicts the lifting of the hardening that has come upon part of Israel, and points out that when this happens, all of Israel will be saved. He conflates Isaiah 45:17 and 59:20a to bolster his argument that God will indeed forgive Israel her sins through the ministry of Jesus. The current state of affairs finds Israel in spiritual hiatus, where her temporary disobedience has allowed the Gentiles entry into grace. Meanwhile, the Jews are still in the running because their fathers were in fact obedient. God doesn't need to change. The only thing that needs to change is Israel's attitude toward her Lord.

Paul makes a distinction between the Gospel and election. The Gospel refers to the propagation of the Good News to the world; a dynamic progression within history. *Election* (NIV) or *choosing*, refers to God's timeless decree about what sort of response he's looking for in his children. The Gospel, subject as it is to man's involvement, is characterized by fits and starts until that which is particular becomes universal. Election, on the other hand, is subject only to God's sovereign will, and it remains inviolate regardless of human response. It's entirely possible, Paul argues, that problems in the first domain do not mean that anything's wrong or changing with regard to the second. God hasn't changed his mind about what he wants, and the patriarchs fulfilled his criteria. That their kids messed up doesn't change the nature of the call or the hope that errant children can reform and find acceptance just like their forebears.

Verse 31 is somewhat convoluted in its logic but is nevertheless very important to understand. Paul argues that just as Gentiles benefitted from the transitory disobedience of the Jews, those same Jews will benefit from the fact that Gentiles are now in God's favor. Eventually Gentiles will bring the Gospel back to the Jews. It's the story of Ruth, being repeated in world history on the scale of all humanity. Naomi went to Gentile lands because of a famine in Israel, and there she became related to and loved by a Gentile woman, Ruth. When the famine was over, Naomi returned to Israel with her daughter-in-law, who then became an integral member of the Jewish community and part of the lineage of the Lord Jesus.[1] Regarding the help Ruth brought Naomi, Boaz said, "May the Lord repay you for what you have done."[2] The witnesses to Ruth's redemption by Boaz said, "May the Lord make the woman who is coming into your home like Rachel and Leah, who together built up the house of Israel. May you have standing in Ephrathah and be famous in Bethlehem. Through the offspring the Lord gives you by this young woman, may your family be like that of Perez, whom Tamar bore to Judah."[3] In addition to being a historical account, the story of Ruth is also a metaphor or prophecy for the passage of the Gospel from Israel to Gentile lands. It is kept alive during a spiritual famine, and then it returns to bear fruit in the land of Israel for eternal redemption.

V. 32

All have, at one time, been disobedient. God, in his love, has redeemed such transgressions and ensured thereby that while one erred, another benefitted. There's not much difference after all between Jew and Gentile.

Doxology [50]

33 O *the* depth
of wealth
and wisdom
and knowledge of God!
How unsearchable his judgments!
and unknowable his ways!
34 "Who has known *the* mind of *the* Lord?
Or who has been his counselor?"
35 "Or who has first given to him, and it will be paid back to him?"
36 For from him and through him and to him *are* all. To him the **glory** into the ages. Amen.

[50] 11:33–36 Three qualities of God, three exclamations, three questions, three relations to God.

1. Matt 1:5.
2. Ruth 2:12.
3. Ruth 4:11–12.

VV. 33–36

This chapter closes with a doxology. A paean to God bursts forth when Paul contemplates the beauty and efficacy of this rather outlandish but brilliant plan to redeem humanity. The problem with special revelation is that by definition it's limited; but you've got to start somewhere. Noah didn't work out, so pick better with Abraham. But by starting with particulars, you must, at some point, graduate to universals. God loves all men and wants them all to be saved.[4] Paul stands awestruck as he realizes that all of human history is finding its fulfillment in his own time and place. Just about everybody is confused, Jew and Gentile alike. Only Paul has had the time and temperament to figure this thing out. He's excited.

4. 1 Tim 2:3; Num 15:15.

Chapter 12

PRÉCIS

Having presented us with his conclusions about how God's plan of redemption operates both in theory and in historical practice, Paul now begins his ascending argument that corresponds with his earlier B section. That section revealed that nobody can generate their own righteousness but must receive it from God. Having established the theoretical principle, Paul now applies it that we might know what we can expect as we live the Christian life. A suitable title is "Life in the Spirit within the church and society." The section extends from 12:1 to 13:14. The Holy Spirit is a person who brings gifts that are intensely practical. The Church has need of our individual gifts, and they also enable us to live successfully in a hostile, pagan world.

Be members of one another, as one body in Anointed, under God's will[51]

Present yourselves to God, do not be conformed to this age

12 I urge you therefore, brothers, by the mercies of God, to present your bodies *as* a living offering—holy, acceptable to God, your thoughtful worship.

2 And do not be conformed to this age,

but be transformed by the renewal of the mind,

that you may discern what *is* God's will—the good and acceptable and perfect.

[51] 12:1—13:14 ABCCBA. Parallel with 3:21—4:25. A's, be transformed; B's, love one another; C's, unity under adversity and diversity, and under God's authorities.

V. 1

As they say, when you read *therefore*, you must see what it's there for. Paul has just finished a very lofty and comprehensive review of God's plan for redeeming a lost and sinful humanity. God has united a humanity divided by race and religion under his son, Jesus Christ. All that God has done for us is now revealed and fully understood. The next step is up to us: What is God looking for by way of response? Do we do something? If so, what? Is there anything we should avoid attempting or doing? All good soteriology includes both God's action and our reaction. Theology leads to pastoral admonition, and theory leads to practice. God has shown us mercy; let us take advantage of that reality.

Living sacrifice. We are to indeed sacrifice ourselves. Not by killing our bodies, which would be suicide, but by killing our self-will. The body lives on, but the motivating force has been altered. We've talked a great deal about worship. Right worship ensures that we remain in God's favor; wrong worship means that we miss out on God's call and become subject to his wrath. What is worship? Right worship, according to Paul, is to *give thanks* to God and to *glorify* him:[1] *thanks* for sacrificing his son for our sins and thereby becoming our Savior and *glorifying* that same son whom we obey as Lord. Glory is accorded to the one who suffers for the welfare of others; Jesus has earned the right to be our Lord through his substitutionary atonement. Right worship is not so much a positive action as much as a negative cessation. We stop running from God, fearful because we are naked.[2] We are now clothed in Christ,[3] and can approach God boldly.[4] Again, there are two ways to get into spiritual trouble with God. One is to deny our sin, the other is to try to reform ourselves by our own strength. In view of all Paul's laid out, both are thoughtless responses. It is better to be thoughtful—both atonement and behavioral reformation must be received vicariously from Christ. To come to this point of surrender results in genuine worship. The form of worship is relatively unimportant; the underlying admission is essential.

V. 2

The number one problem we have is spiritual; our spirit lies dead until animated by the incoming Holy Spirit of Jesus. The second problem we face is

1. Rom 1:21.
2. Gen 3:10.
3. 2 Cor 5:3; Gal 3:27.
4. Heb 4:16.

that our minds are deluded, and our thinking is darkened. The ideal is that when we are baptized in the Holy Spirit, we erase all our prior conceptions and conclusions and let God open our minds to truth based on the ministry of Jesus. This is not an easy task; it took Paul years in Arabia to reform his thinking.[5] When the mind is renewed, behavioral transformation can then take place. Our bodies are important; Jesus sanctified the body when he became incarnate. God has a will for us that was realized in the Garden but perverted by the Fall. God's will has never altered, and when we are restored to our proper orientation—spirit over mind, mind over body—it becomes possible to not only know God's will, but to do it. The lie of the Devil is that when we do God's will, it's somehow odious to us. When we are born again, our will becomes his will, and we find it to be good, acceptable, and perfect.[6]

Be united in Anointed under God who has given us different gifts[52]

3 I say, by the grace given to me, to every one among you,
not to think *of yourself* more highly than you ought to think,
but to think soberly
as to each God has apportioned a measure of faithfulness.
4 For as in one body many members we have,
and all the members do not have the same function,
5 so the many, one body we are in Anointed, and each one members of one another.
6 Having gifts differing according to the grace given to us, *let us use them*:
if prophecy, in the proportion of the faithfulness;
7 if service, in the serving;
if the teacher, in the teaching;
8 if the encourager, in the encouragement;
the giver, in liberality;
the leader, in diligence;
the compassionate, in cheerfulness;
9 the love, without hypocrisy;
hating the evil;
holding on to the good;

5. Gal 1:17.

6. Oswald Chambers says, "When you are rightly related to God, it is a life of freedom and liberty and delight, you *are* God's will, and all your common-sense decisions are His will for you unless He checks." Chambers, *My Utmost*, March 20.

10 in brotherly love, one another loving;
in honor, one another preferring;
11 in diligence, not lacking;
in the spirit, fervent;
in the Lord, serving;
12 in hope, rejoicing;
in hardship, enduring;
in prayer, persevering;
13 to the needs of the holy *ones,* contributing;
to hospitality, being diligent.

[52] 12:3—13 Be united in Anointed under God who has given us different gifts, with a list of 20 instructions for unity, centering on love. Parallel with 13:8–10, love your neighbor.

V. 3

When Paul talks of the grace given him, he's actually saying that he is speaking for the Lord. More specifically, it is the Lord speaking through him. It's his badge of authentication. The danger of telling people that God resides in them in a very real way, is that they get puffed up and start dictating to others. Many people join the church because it's the one place where they can find affirmation and purpose. This is good, but the flip side of every good thing is the potential for something bad, and no sooner does Paul say the good about God working in and through us, than he tackles the sequitur of lay popery.

VV. 4–5

Paul uses the human body as an analogy for the organization of the church. The human body is diverse though integrated, and in this way is just like the church. The church needs to accomplish a variety of functions. God, being a God of order and beauty, has given skills to the various members in view of what the entire church needs to accomplish. There will be skills designed to minister to the members of the body and other skills designed to minster to those who are not yet members. There are certain maintenance functions, and there are others that focus outward toward the larger world.

VV. 6–8

Here is a litany of divine gifts, each followed by the means of putting them to practical use. *Grace*. When Jesus lives in us, his presence and overarching power are manifested in different ways. God loves variety. That's why he's made people different colors, different genders, speaking different languages, and developing different cultures. Jesus is anything but monochromatic. Perhaps his preference for variety is because he is looking for *syndouloi*, coworkers. The church is his bride, and she is to learn to exercise her regency in this world before his return, his *parousia*. He does the heavy lifting, but he enjoys letting his grace be filtered and caressed by our personalities as it comes forth. In our relationship with Christ, we lose our individuality but maintain our personality. The former is a remnant of the Fall, the latter is an enduring gift from our Creator.

Prophecy. This is not predicting the future but rather pronouncing God's perspective on a particular situation. Because prophecy involves receiving revelation from God, it will necessarily be in proportion to the experience the individual has in walking with the Lord. It's easy to get what God says wrong, as he speaks with a still, small voice.[7] Too often today, "prophetic voice" has become code for critical and unloving condemnation. Paul felt it was the most important gift for the congregation because it contained actionable information from the seat of God.

Service. This is an anachronism in today's world. Service often means doing what somebody else wants, whether it's good or bad. Service in the church means doing what's necessary for daily living and ministry to proceed. It's often unseen and unheralded, but nonetheless necessary and of high value in God's eyes. Genuine service is done not for the person, but for Jesus himself. He says we'll be judged by how we served, or failed to serve, other Christians.[8]

Teaching here means Christian catechesis. There is propositional truth in Christianity, and our faith is supposed to be founded upon both heavenly and historical facts. God gave us minds, and much of what we need to know about God and ourselves is unchanging and is intended to be learned and passed down to succeeding generations. Christianity does not need to be reinvented. The idiom may change, but the content does not. Christians have historically been the only group who, for the simple love of knowledge, have kept science, facts, and learning alive during times of cultural decline. Even

7. 1 Kgs 19:12, or *gentle whisper* (NIV).

8. Matt 25:31–46.

the classics of pagan culture were preserved by Christians who felt that all intellectual endeavors were worth consideration.

Encouragement. Who doesn't need it? When I contemplate the glum faces of people in public, I'm reminded that most of them are doing their best and just barely hanging on. Think of the amount of energy it takes to shop for food, cook a meal, clean the house, wash clothes, balance a checkbook, raise children, discipline them, and care for crazy or ailing family members. In Alaska during winter, more time is spent getting ready to venture outside and recover from having been outside than is ever spent outside. Daily life is preparation, execution, and reparation. Who doesn't appreciate a gesture of personal appreciation for the efforts they put forth every day? In the church, it's viewed as an actual ministry.

Contributing to the needs of others (NIV). The NIV goes all flowery on this one; actual translation: *the giver*. The basis of all giving is the recognition of another's need as outstripping our own. Two things are necessary for true Christian giving. First of all, the giver must have something to give. The church used to be the only established source of welfare, but this function, like so many others, has been usurped by the state. This is unfortunate, because income redistribution is no longer voluntary, but compulsory. Secondly, there must be genuine need on the part of the recipient., and the state lacks the spiritual sensitivity to make this determination. When a person is in financial distress, it's sometimes because God has withheld his blessings in order to get their attention. To fill their need without consulting God is to insult God and hurt the needy. Genuine needs exist, and the church is the only organ for meeting those needs in God's economy. When the government takes charity, health care, and education away from the church, all Christians are left with is talking about what happens when we die. God intends charity and relief to be used to relieve genuine human suffering and to manifest the love of God for the lost. The Scriptures teach that although we cannot control our wayward hearts, we can control our finances, and the heart always follows money.[9]

Leader in diligence. This implies consistent attention to the welfare of those put in our charge. People need to be led. In our Lord's own words, we're like sheep without a shepherd. Left to ourselves, we wander off and get into trouble. The leader knows this and is not surprised by it. He makes himself available to, in the words of St. Peter, reward the good and punish the wicked.[10] This is true in the church no less than in the polity. Leadership relies upon the power of good ideas and personal integrity.

9. Matt 6:21; Luke 12:34.

10. 1Pet 2:14.

Showing mercy (NIV) or being *compassionate* is a very difficult task. On the one hand there's the temptation of entering into another's suffering so completely that both are overwhelmed and there is no recovery. On the other hand, it's never possible for a person to know the depths of another's suffering, and superficial gestures can be unhelpful and actively annoying. *Cheerfulness* is the best remedy; in the end, everything will work out. This life is not all there is, and someday we'll be in a world where everybody agrees that Jesus is Lord and there is no more suffering or crying. Until then, we need as much laughter as any situation allows. Jesus laughed, a lot. Perspective allows—demands—mirth.

VV. 9–13

Paul now moves from what distinguishes Christians in their common life to behavioral guidelines that apply to individual Christians. While some specialize and have extraordinary gifts, all Christians are to manifest good behavior. We operate best in groups, but we are often left alone to manifest Christ to a broken and lost world. To that end, there are some absolutes. Sincerity ensures that love is coming from Jesus in us to others, and not some counterfeit of human origin. *Hate what is evil* (NIV). People say Christians are not supposed to hate. This is baloney. Of course we're to hate—even hate is a gift of God. Hate and fear are related, and there's plenty to fear in the world. David would say, "Gusts of anger seize me as I think of evil men who forsake thy law (NIV)."[11] Christians are supposed to hate passionately, but selectively. Evil hurts not only people, but the Lord who made them.

Cling to what is good (NIV). It is not up to us to decide what's good and evil. That's what got Adam and Eve into trouble; they took this honor—and burden—upon themselves. We are to let God decide what's evil and what's good, and then avoid the one while clinging to the other. Goodness is a reflection of God himself, and his Word cannot be understood as anything other than an exposition of all that is good, and by contrast, all that is not good. Value judgments are dependent upon an absolute standard that is extrinsic to human experience.

Brotherly love. This is *philadelphia*. Our word *love* falls short of the nuances of the several Greek words that we translate as love. Because all people have God as their Father, they are ipso facto brothers. The Indian chief Red Jacket or Keeper Awake makes this point when addressing a Christian missionary.[12] When you become a Christian, you join a family. We all came

11. Ps 119:53 (NEB).

12. "The Great Spirit has made us all, but he has made a great difference between his

from families of varying functionality. No matter how good or bad your family of origin was, the church can and should be better.

Honor others in preference to yourself (NIV). Honor is rare today. Soldiers still have it, and most police do too. It's the idea that we subscribe to a code of thought and behavior that we have received from outside ourselves, and we let it guide us without the need of supervision. When we see somebody who has no need of punishment or threat of discovery, who does the right thing simply because it's the right thing, this person deserves to be honored. Salute the flag, stand at attention, shut up when others speak, listen to what they say, and try to be like them. Stand for something greater than yourself.

Diligence or *zeal* (NIV). How many people get excited about something besides sports? God loves diligent people, who persevere, and zealous people, who have a passion for something. Things matter, even little things. A man who owned a portable toilet business insisted a developer inspect one of his toilets. The developer demurred, but eventually relented to repeated entreaties. The thing was spotless. "I clean them," said the first, "as if Jesus were going to use them."

The NIV links the ideas of *zeal*, being *fervent* and *serving* the Lord. This is probably Paul's intent. All we do is to serve him. What lasts, if not things that resonate in eternity? When we invest in the Lord's activities, we are doing something permanent. We all search for significance; that's why young men go to war and old men go to church. We need to be part of something bigger than ourselves. We will all serve somebody. What a privilege to be a part of *his* enterprises.

Joyful, patient, faithful (NIV). *Rejoicing, enduring, persevering*. These words are about work. Is it natural to be rejoicing because of an unseen future, enduring in spite of hardships, persevering in prayer that may seem pointless? Of course not, but the scandal of Christianity is that through the ministry of the Spirit we are able to disassociate ourselves from the immediate, the pressing, the actual, the now, and see that these things are really chimeras. There is a more sure, reliable, guaranteed reality that will eventually trump current circumstances. We are not insane; we are fully grounded in a reality that has been foretold and purchased for us by Another. The Christian is the most sane person in the world, because we are banking not on what is, but what is to come. The only catch is, it takes effort to see with eyes and hear with ears that are not deceived by the intensity of the present.

---

white and red children." Quoted by Nathaniel Coverly. Society, *Brief Account*, Portfolio 47, Folder 25.

Who does not have a saint who was instrumental in our conversion? These are the *holy ones* who precede us and who equip us to become holy ones to others. Christianity is a chain of generations. People to come will not know of these mysteries unless we prove faithful and do our part to pass truth on. Saints have practical needs like anyone else, and we should be conscientious in meeting them. Why do Christian parachurch ministries not have pension plans and health insurance? Why do the Saints not merit what secular businesses deem essential? Find a holy man, find out his needs, and give to his relief. It may be done for you some day.

Hospitality in the Near East is not only a duty, it is an art. After the bedroom, the dining table is the next most intimate activity we can share with others. Note how Lot's host valued the honor of his guest.[13] When are we weaker than when we are out of house and home, at the mercy of the larger world? It is often the unexpected guest who brings not only hunger and fatigue, but a message of hope and reassurance from a lofty God. They say Billy Sunday took an offering from a community, but he left something else, something greater.[14]

Unity under adversity and diversity (20 more instructions)

14 Bless the persecutors,
    bless
and do not curse.
    15 . . . to rejoice with *the* rejoicing,
        to weep with *the* weeping,
    16 the same regard for one another having,
    not proud being,
        but with the lowly associating,
    do not be conceited.
    17 No one evil for evil repaying;
        taking thought for what is good in the sight of all;
    18 if possible, on your part, living peaceably with all;
    19 not yourselves avenging, beloved;
        but give place to *God's* vengeance;
    for it is written: "Mine *is* vengeance, I will repay, says *the* Lord."
    20 Rather, "if your enemy is hungry, feed him;
        if he is thirsty, give drink to him;

13. Gen 19:8.

14. Sunday left " . . . a trail of sober homes and debt paying people from El Paso to Texarkana." *The Congregationalist*, 274.

for *by* doing this you will heap burning coals on his head."
21 Do not be overcome by the evil,
but overcome the evil with the good.

V. 14

We know little of persecution today. There are people who have been sued, arrested, and fired for being Christians, but these are the exceptions in our country.[15] Other places, it's much more common.[16] Those who are persecuted or otherwise hurt by the deliberate actions of others are enjoined to bless and not curse. Those who can obey this command can move on from their trials and forge new lives and ministries. Those who cannot forgive tend to be locked into the past and are dominated by recriminations. Though it has its own perverse attraction, nursing wounds hurts the victim more than the perpetrator.

V. 15

We are encouraged to go beyond empathy to a genuine sympathy with others. We are not to merely to join in their feelings, but in the expression of their feelings. It's been observed that this kind of emotional union doubles the joys and halves the miseries of life. Spiritual awareness makes us better friends, better people. The person who is not beset with their own problems has the ability to help others who are.

V. 16

Paul urges harmonious living, then tells us how to do it. Pride and conceit are poison in any relationship, and Paul proscribes them. Class distinctions are being erased in modern American society, but Christian churches tend

15. e.g. Jack Phillips of Masterpiece Cakeshop. Additionally, I know an Episcopal priest who was accused of financial malfeasance by his own bishop because the priest opposed the revisionist sexual agenda being adopted by the larger Episcopal church. After losing his parish building, his own home, and being inhibited to operate as a priest, he was subsequently exonerated in a criminal court proceeding. He prays for his persecutors, as Paul urges us to do.

16. I've met a man who was thrown into prison in Morocco for evangelizing the citizens. In prison, he led a Muslim man to Christ on the eve of the latter's execution. Finally, my friend was escorted to the border and deported. The warden said that if he were kept in prison any longer, all the prisoners would be converted.

to lag behind in this regard. Congregations that emphasize racial, cultural, and sociological diversity often struggle to establish a cohesive family identity. On the one hand we're to welcome people from any and all situations. On the other hand, there's a natural tendency to gravitate towards gatherings that are more homogeneous. Balance should be sought, and freedom should be extended to those with differing tastes and needs.

V. 17

Don't repay *evil* for evil. This is directly opposed to the Mosaic justice of an eye for an eye, etc.[17] Jesus had already introduced this novel idea, and Paul is merely repeating what Jesus said.[18] In human terms, not retaliating is a sign of weakness; for the Christian, it's a sign of strength. What allows us to rise above the tit for tat mandated by the world is a twofold conviction. First of all, we know that vengeance is the Lord's, and eventually all will be set right without our help. Secondly, a willingness to suffer is a sure and certain sign that we have something the perpetrator doesn't, and as such is a springboard for effective evangelism. People who are doing wrong know full well what they're up to. When we evince deeper character than they, they are almost forced to inquire about our source of strength. Suffering is a call to intercession, not judgment.

V. 18

Peaceably (NIV). Peace is not an absence of conflict, it's the presence of agreement on fundamentals. Peace can only be achieved through the eradication of evil. Paul qualifies this injunction with *if possible, on your part*, or *if it is possible, as far as it depends on you* (NIV), because sometimes it's not wholly dependent upon us, or always possible, to live at peace. Take war, for example, or dealing with those who threaten the civil order. The type and severity of the conflict are dependent upon the least moral, least ethical player in the dispute. Sometimes the greater evil is to wait, to temporize, to appease; witness Hitler in his adventures prior to WWII. What could have been solved with a limited police action when he annexed the Rhineland, later required the death of 50 or 60 million people to set right. Paul's qualification is important. Quakers and the Swiss claim to take the moral high road by not participating in war, but they are unknowingly joining the side

17. Exod 21:24.

18. Matt 5:38–42.

of the biggest bully, for it's he who benefits from their lack of resistance. Don't seek conflict, but take the long view when it comes to ensuring a lasting peace. The soldier is the most Christ-like figure in society, for he puts himself in danger to ensure the safety of others. Pacifists are, in the words of George Patton, either "crackpots" or "sophists."[19]

V. 19

Vengeance or *revenge* (NIV) is something besides the legitimate maintenance of order and decorum. It implies that we're somehow getting even, inflicting on the perpetrator a measure of their own abuse. This is very attractive from a carnal perspective, and it titillates us as we contemplate the possibilities for getting even. However, Paul points out that in exacting revenge, we're trespassing on God's domain. Only God is morally pure, only God sees the whole picture, only God knows what's best for the sinner, and only God can come to our aid as a victim. When we interpose our efforts to even things out, we do three things. First of all, we lose any moral advantage we had in the beginning. We cannot evangelize when we're no better than the other person. Secondly, God withholds his own remedies when we take over. God may let the bad guy off the hook when we get involved. Finally, we become guilty of the same sin we're trying to condemn.[20] As we point out the errors of others, we reveal that we, too, have the capacity to know and commit the same acts.

V. 20

Paul dilates on his theme of avoiding revenge by quoting Proverbs 25:21. Not only are we to avoid the negative, but we're to actively pursue the positive. By acting in the best interests of the sinner, we transform the entire exchange, and enable God to bring good from bad. First of all, the burning coals are guilt and self-consciousness on the part of the perpetrator who sees his position as morally inferior. We cannot deny him this experience. Secondly, evil feasts on truth. The Enemy doesn't tempt us with lies, he tempts us with genuine facts of injustice and hatred. If the Enemy can get us looking backwards in life at all the injustices and slights we've received, he has succeeded. By not availing ourselves to our rights—and indeed serving those who hurt us—we can orient ourselves not to the slavery of the past,

19. Quoted by Allen, *Lucky Forward*, 23.

20. Rom 2:1.

but to the unlimited possibilities of the future. Evil can only be overcome when somebody is willing to stop the vicious circle of attack and retribution. A willingness to suffer when it's wise and necessary is the surest sign of God's presence in us.

V. 21

Life is characterized by conflict. We can't avoid conflict, but we can decide which side we're going to be on. To not make a decision is to make a decision—a bad one. Bailey's translation has the definite article *the* associated with evil. This is right, for evil is animate, active, and monolithic. There is one Source of all evil, with the goal to kill, steal, and destroy.[21] Don't worry about which side will demand less of you, decide which side is going to win and will pay everlasting dividends.

21. John 10:10.

Chapter 13

PRÉCIS

This chapter constitutes the second half of a B section as we ascend from the general conclusions of Paul's letter to a complement of what he wrote in chapters 3 and 4. As such, it is an application of the theory he's gone to such lengths to establish in chapter 12. Here he moves from the personal behavior required of those who call themselves Christians to their proper behavior in society. This is a critical point because the civil authorities he now talks about may well be the persecutors he spoke of at the end of chapter 12.The force of his argument is all the more compelling if this is true. The natural reaction we have to persecutors is to despise and resist them. For Paul to say we are not to resist, and in fact submit to authorities who abuse their power, is probably a first in the study of human polity. Christians are, among other things, to make great citizens. In order to underscore this stunning position, he constructs an extended chiasmus in verses 1–7. Associated verses are paired to show their relationship.

Unity under God's authorities and ministers (religious and civil)

13 Every soul must submit to governing authorities.

For there is no authority except from God, and those that exist have been established by God.

2 Accordingly, whoever resists the authority, God's ordinance opposes,

and those who oppose will get condemnation on themselves.

3 For rulers are not a terror to good conduct, but to evil.

Do you wish to have no fear of the authority?

Do the good,

and you will receive its approval,
4 for it is God's servant to you
for good.
But if you do evil, be afraid,
for it does not wear the sword for nothing,
for it is God's servant, to take vengeance on the evildoer.
5 Therefore, *it is* a necessity to be subject, not only because of vengeance, but also because of conscience.
6 This is why you also pay taxes, for they are God's ministers, devoting themselves to this very thing.
7 Pay to all their dues, tax to whom tax *is due*, custom to whom custom, respect to whom respect, honor to whom honor.

VV. 1A, 7

Every soul. Not some or even most, but every soul is included. We all are to pay all our taxes, as well as obligations of custom, respect, and honor.

VV. 1B, 6

This injunction applies to all secular authorities, as they are, one and all, ordained by God. You think they're just a bunch of politicians and civil servants, bureaucrats, but they are in fact ministers of God, devoting themselves full time to the public welfare. One of the greatest misunderstandings about human nature is that we're inherently good and don't need to be restrained. We're not, and we do. Worse than oppression is a power vacuum, where there is anarchy. Witness what has happened when oppressive regimes have been toppled, only to result in worse chaos and suffering than before. Look at Weimar Germany in the early 20th century, or Viet Nam, South Africa, Iraq or Afghanistan in the latter half. What happens when the power goes out or the police are detained, even in the USA?

VV. 2A, 5

God makes no distinction between direct opposition to himself or his agents. Not only does the offender risk punishment from the civil authority, he also risks punishment from God himself. Our common sense tells us that transgression leads to civil consequences; our conscience tells us that there will also be spiritual consequences.

VV. 2B, 4E

This condemnation is directly from God, even though it may be filtered through the agency of human authorities. It's actual vengeance from God, which goes beyond justice and takes the form of punitive action. When Jesus returned to destroy the disobedient Jewish nation, temple, and religion in AD 70, he did so through the agency of the Roman Empire and General Titus. Appearances are deceiving, as it was none other than Christ himself, coming on the clouds.[1]

VV. 3A, 4D

Today there's much talk about police misconduct, and in a few cases—in the low double digits—this may be true. But in view of the half million encounters between police and alleged felons each year, this figure is statistically insignificant. What is our attitude towards the police? Do we recoil and think about what we're doing wrong that might attract their attention, or do we welcome their presence, knowing they're there to protect us? Peter points out that the role of government is to reward the good and punish the transgressor.[2] Luther dilates on this theme to our advantage.[3]

VV. 3B, 4C

Again, our reaction to authority belies our behavior. If we're good, we have nothing to fear, but if we're not good, then we would do well to fear. Abusive authority is an exception, but the general rule applies, according to Paul, even in cases of unjust persecution.

1. Matt 24:30; 26:64; Mark 13:26; 14:62; Rev 1:7.

2. 1 Pet 2:14.

3. "... God did not put a useless piece of paper into the emperor's hand, but rather the hardest and sharpest sword with which to execute punishment; not a pen, but a sword. God gave the emperor a sword to indicate that civil government is not to forgive but rather to use the edge of the sword to punish crimes." Luther, *Sermons of Martin Luther*, 131.

VV. 3C, 4B

The theme is *good*. God wants it, and so does his servant the civil authority. They are on the same side, and we can't despise the one and not the other. Civil authority can go wrong, and in certain circumstances armed rebellion is justified. These cases are few and far between, and they must be undertaken in the context of obedience to God.

VV. 3D–4A

This is the conclusion of the chiasmus and the purpose of the whole argument. Our regard for civil authorities is a reflection of our piety, and the authority's approval can be understood as God's approval. It's easy for a criminal to ask God to forgive him, but much harder to accept society's punishment and thereby receive society's forgiveness. We can't ask God to forgive us and not tell man about it as well. Refuse your punishment in this life, and you'll have to pay in the life to come.[4] When Jesus tells us to be reconciled to our adversaries " . . . on the way," he means while we yet live.[5]

Love your neighbor

8 Owe no one anything,

    except one another to love,

    for one who loves the other

has fulfilled *the* law.

        9 The "Do no adultery, Do not murder, Do not steal, Do not desire," and any other commandment,

            are summed up in this word:

        "Love your neighbor as yourself."

10 Love

    does no wrong to the neighbor;

    fulfillment of *the* law, therefore,

is love.

V. 8

This appears to be a new subject, but the idea of debt is a continuation of the prior obligations owed to civil authorities, which include taxes. Pay your

4. Matt 5:26; Luke 12:59.
5. Matt 5:25.

taxes. You don't have to pay more than you owe, but you do have to pay what you owe. Cheating on taxes is a great way to grieve the Holy Spirit and inhibit his operation in our lives. Other debts are similar in that payment is a form of worship.[6]

Sometimes this verse is used to say you can't buy things on credit. Buying on credit has its own problems, but this is not what the verse is talking about. The issue is not owing *per se*, but withholding that which is legitimately owed to others when we have the obligation and means to pay. Consumer debt keeps the economy humming, but also leads to personal problems and demand-pull inflation. Why not wait for gratification? It won't kill you, and it may give God time to provide from his own largesse.

We have a continuing obligation to let God love others through us. It's an obligation for two reasons. First, we have to love because God loved us. It's only good manners. Second, it's work. The constant temptation is to let our flesh react to others and love them under our own steam. This strategy soon fails and in humility we have to give God permission to love others through us. The mystery of why God allows birth defects, accidents and decrepitude may be better appreciated if we view these events as opportunities to manifest supernatural love. These people and situations keep us honest. The Law is largely negative: don't do this or that. Love is positive: it seeks opportunities to do good to others in a way a negation cannot.

VV. 9–10

Of the Ten Commandments, only two are positive directives; the other eight are proscriptions. Paul quotes four of the latter to show the contrast between prohibitions of Law and the positive endorsement of love. They mean the same thing, but the Law is imposed from without whereas love is released from within. What Paul is really saying is that those who still live under the Law, Jews, have a harder time being good citizens and neighbors. Where they have to work and slave and worry about trespasses, the Christian who is an avenue for the Holy Spirit can forget all that and let the Lord do the work. Judaism doesn't work in theory, nor does it work in practice. Getting along with your neighbor is worship, too.

6. I was sold a generator, and upon my arrival home, I realized they had undercharged me $200 by selling me the wrong model. I returned to the store, explained their error, and paid the difference. An acquaintance who once boarded a bus was given too much change by the operator. The rider returned to the operator and explained the mistake. The driver said, "I deliberately gave you too much. I knew you claimed to be a Christian, and I wanted to see if you really were."

Throw off the works of darkness, put on the Anointed

11 Besides this, knowing the time, that now *is the* hour for you to wake from sleep,

for now salvation *is* nearer to us than when we believed.

12 The night has advanced,

the day is at hand.

Let us then throw off the works of darkness.

Let us put on the armor of light.

13 Let us walk properly as in *the* day,

not in orgies and drunkenness, not in promiscuity and indecency, not in rivalry and jealousy.

14 But put on the Lord Jesus Anointed,

and make no provision for desires of the flesh.

11–14

A very important chiasmus concludes this chapter, as it deals with the nature of the response God is looking for from his children. The first part speaks of the imperative to respond; the second half deals with the nature of that response.

It's important to remember that if the first problem the church faced was the basis for including Gentiles, the second problem was the delayed *parousia* of the Lord. All the Biblical writers, including Paul, appear to expect his return at any moment. Only Peter seems to view the event as variable and dependent upon the maturity of the church.[7] Imminence demands attention, and a godly response to God's Grace is called for. Is this not what separates all Christian communions, sects, and denominations, but a fundamental disagreement about what God is looking for? Roman Catholics say it is membership in their church and obedience to its dictates. Baptists and other fundamentalists say we're saved by the fun and indulgence we do not partake of. Reformed Christians say it's not up to us at all, and any response from us is mandated by God without the option of disobedience on our part. Dispensationalists say salvation depends on knowledge of dates and times. Which, if any, of these people are right? Clearly, God is indeed looking for a response, and those who do not respond are likened to those who sleep. We are to awaken, because time is advancing. Even though in retrospect we can see that the church is immature and Christ, in his love for his bride, tarries, what Paul says is true of the individual. Each moment

7. 2 Pet 3:11b–12a.

we are closer to our own death, and the brevity of life is what gives it value. Now is a time for moral agency; now we can formulate our spiritual destiny, which upon death becomes fixed.[8]

Like John in his Gospel, Paul equates physical darkness with spiritual ignorance. In terms of both human history and personal conversion, *night* refers to when Jesus was unknown and the flesh reigned supreme. With the coming of the Gospel, to both society and the individual, spiritual revelation is equated with physical light. Just as the day follows the night, Jesus dispels the darkness and brings vision and understanding. What is God looking for by way of response? Verses 12 c–d give us the answer. It is the conclusion of the chiasmus. We have to *throw off* the deeds of *darkness*. Our role is *negative*, to let go of that to which we cling that grieves the Holy Spirit. When we persist in sin, we recommit Adam's sin and render the Holy Spirit impotent to come to our aid. By giving up our right to ourselves, we say, in effect, that the first Adam no longer speaks for us, and we are now open to the ministry of the second Adam. This is what Paul means when he says throw off.[9]

Further, we are to *put on*, in this case, *armor*. Armor is a passive, defensive proposition. You wear armor to protect you from injury brought by an enemy. Our armor is Christ, in terms both of the protection he affords from moral condemnation by virtue of his death on the Cross, and also from the power he imbues in us when he dwells in the seat of our will: our hearts. He does the work; we do not. Our role is passive; he is the actor. *Light* in this case refers to the whole spectrum of positive qualities it implies: perception, revelation, understanding, public display, endless possibility, and Christ himself.

Notice how sinners prefer night to hide their misdeeds. Even the most brazen sinners have limits about how far they will go in disclosing their misdeeds. A good gauge of behavior is this: would I be proud to do this in public? Another is this: what if everybody were to do it? Paul zeroes in on six behaviors that cannot tolerate the light of public inspection. Note that three have to do with sex. It was a problem then, and it's a problem today. *Orgies* are self-explanatory, designating group drinking leading to indiscriminate sex. *Drunkenness*. What is Paul's attitude towards alcohol? Does he have a

8. Luke 16:26; Heb 9:27.

9. Oswald Chambers explains our role in our salvation: "Have you made the following decision about sin—that it must be completely killed in you? It takes a long time to come to the point of making this complete and effective decision about sin. It is, however, the greatest moment in your life once you decide that sin must die in you—not simply be restrained, suppressed, or counteracted, but crucified—just as Jesus Christ died for the sin of the world." Chambers, *My Utmost*, April 10.

zero-tolerance policy, like many Christian sects? Clearly, he does not.[10] Nor does Jesus. Jesus made 180 gallons of the finest wine ever—just how big was that wedding? Paul is talking about drinking to excess, to the point where the liquid spirit interferes with the Holy Spirit. *Promiscuity* refers to having sexual contact with people to whom we are not married. Remember when that was wrong? It used to be illegal. *Indecency* probably refers to homosexual activity. That, too, used to be unacceptable.

Rivalry and jealousy. In many ways our society actually endorses these related emotions. Rivals seek advantage at the expense of another; this clearly militates against Paul's admonition to love others, even those who hurt us. Jealousy means we can't rejoice in the success of others with whom we compete. Rather than adopt a jealous attitude, Paul has already told us to rejoice with those who rejoice. It's a divine rule that when one prospers, all prosper. This is true in church but also in economics. It took 18 centuries of Christian influence for Adam Smith to promulgate the basic principles of free market capitalism and in doing so repudiate the crude, pagan system of mercantilism.

Put on or *clothe* (NIV). The final act of the convert is to put Jesus on as a garment. Nakedness used to be okay in the Garden, before man rebelled and lost his innocence. It was on account of nakedness that Adam was afraid and ran from God. Just as Pentecost and tongues reversed the curse of Babel, here Paul gives remedy to our fundamental nakedness before God. We approach him boldly because now we are clothed in Christ.[11] Just as his blood covers our sins, his life covers our incapacity and weakness. There is a corollary to putting on Christ, which is that we make no provision for the *desires of the flesh*. The desires of the flesh wage war against the soul,[12] because they compete for the same real estate in our hearts. Demons derive worship when we show allegiance to anyone or anything but Christ. The flesh is noble because it was made by God, and it is holy because Jesus had a body. But it is only noble and holy when it's not in charge. It's a means to an end, and the end is dictated by the Spirit within us.

10. 1 Tim 5:23.

11. Gal 3:27.

12. 1 Pet 2:11.

Chapter 14

PRÉCIS

This chapter brings us to the last section of the letter, an A component that bookends the introduction that extended from 1:1 to 3:20. A suitable title is "Potential cultural conflicts between Jew and Gentile." As Paul is concluding his letter, he must admonish his audience—both Jew and Gentile—that their theological equality laid out at the beginning of his message will not prevent cultural friction. Though they are unified in God's eyes, they must strive to exhibit that unity in day-to-day living. This will affect how they eat, worship, and of course, drink alcohol. The modern church would do well to reread Romans 14.

Jews and Gentiles, glorify God together, as brothers
Welcome your weak brother (a Jew) as God has welcomed him

14 Welcome the weak in faith, but not for disputes over opinions.
2 One has faith to eat everything, another who is weak eats vegetables.
3 The one who eats must not despise the one who does not eat, and
the one who does not eat must not judge the one who eats,
for God has welcomed him.
4 Who are you to judge a servant of another?
To his own Lord he stands or falls.
And he will be upheld, for the Lord is able to make him stand.
5 One esteems one day above another,
another esteems every day.
Each should be fully convinced in his own mind.

6 Whoever observes the day, observes *it* for *the* Lord.

And whoever eats, eats for *the* Lord, for he gives thanks to God;

and whoever does not eat, abstains for *the* Lord and gives thanks to God.

7 None of us lives to oneself, and no one dies to oneself.

8 For if we live, we live to the Lord, and if we die, we die to the Lord.

So whether we live or whether we die, we are the Lord's.

9 For this Anointed died and lived, that he may be Lord of both *the* dead and *the* living.

10 You then, why do you judge your brother? Or you, why do you look down on your brother?

For we will all stand before God's judgment seat.

11 For it is written: "*As* I live, says *the* Lord, to me will bow every knee, and every tongue will praise God."

12 So each of us will give account of oneself.

13 Therefore let us no longer judge one another.

V. 1

Paul continues his admonitions about how Christians should behave, now with regard to people who are already converted but whose faith has yet to impart good sense. Remember, we're not saved because of how much we know or how accurate our doctrine is. God cares a great deal more about the humility of our heart and the general cast of our behavior than our doctrine. Doctrine is important, but ultimately, it's a means to an end, not an end in itself. Paul is being nice when he describes people who don't have much discernment or sense as having weak faith. There are many, many things open to dispute, things that God may or may not have an opinion about, but about which people certainly do have opinions. These are *adiaphora*, what Paul calls *disputable matters* (NIV).

V. 2

Food is a touchy subject for Jew and Gentile alike. The Jew has been given a long list of things they are not allowed to eat.[1] Gentiles, for their part, often

1. e.g. Lev 11.

dedicated their meat to gods before eating. In a society where eating has strong social and religious overtones, it was often hard to reconcile competing sensibilities. Paul has just been arguing that Jews and Gentiles are equal in God's sight, and now he must translate what he has explained in theological terms into practical policies. That people with weak faith eat only vegetables is apparently nothing new. Those who avoid meat on moral grounds can take comfort that before the Fall, there was no death and therefore no meat eating. Since that time, we've been given permission to eat meat, and we can follow Jesus' example in doing so.

V. 3

On any given day, Jews and Gentiles might have occasion to eat or avoid certain foods. This is the background for Paul's admonition that there be no judgment about who's eating what. Note that the Jerusalem Council decided that the only dietary restrictions that should be placed on Gentile converts were that they should not eat food sacrificed to idols, blood, or the meat of animals that had been strangled. The first was intended to steer them away from empty religious practices, and the latter two were designed to keep them from revolting any Jews who might be present. The general message is that all the dietary fussiness of the past, for Jew and Gentile alike, has been replaced with a whole new system where righteousness proceeds from God to anyone who has been identified with Jesus in his death and resurrection.

V. 4

Here's the point Paul's driving at. We each belong to the Lord and function as his servant. What counts is what the master thinks, not what the other servants think. We can safely ignore the performance of other servants, because it really doesn't involve us. We should worry about our own performance—whether we're doing what we've been told to do or not do. The salvation of others is Jesus' problem, and in saving people he's overcome much greater issues than what they do or don't eat. Think of the enormity of our sin and rebellion, all that Jesus bore on the Cross. What we eat is important to the extent it is healthy, but it shouldn't carry symbolic meaning.

VV. 5–6A

Paul moves from talking about food to talking about ritual observances found on the calendar. The Jews were big on the Sabbath, the seventh day. Christians preferred to worship on the first day, Sunday, the day of the Resurrection. And pagans had their holidays too. Get them together and you've got a recipe for conflict. We still have Seventh Day Adventists and others who have gone back to Saturday worship as opposed to Sunday. The Western Church argued about the date of Easter until the Synod of Whitby, then took up the fight with the Eastern Church which continues to this day. Paul says what counts is not the actual day, but the heart attitude of the worshipper. If they're doing it for the Lord, then details don't matter.

V. 6B

Paul returns to food. Again, the point is that when we eat food or fast from food, and we invoke the Lord, it's worship. Little gestures please the Lord, like when we refuse to indulge in some pleasure we're perfectly entitled to, simply as a sign of our appreciation for him. When we give up our rights it's going against the grain of our society, and it marks us as a breed apart. Jesus didn't say if you fast, but *when* you fast.[2]

VV. 7–9

In order to show how trivial and inane the discussion of food and feast days is, Paul escalates the debate and talks about the big issue of death. What we are worried about is what happens while we live, yet have we thought about the ordeal death represents? Jesus came to redeem us from sin and spiritual separation from God. Shouldn't that miracle be what occupies our every waking thought? We can have confidence in our daily lives because Jesus lived successfully, died on purpose, and rose again to validate our redemption. He also reigns and directs us individually, so we can relax—relax about our own behavior and also the behavior of others.

VV. 10–13A

Paul continues. We can conclude that word had reached him that the Roman congregation was having trouble with the basics of Christian fellowship.

2. Matt 6:16; Luke 4:35.

We've got a tough task ahead, and that is to justify every thought and word to the shepherd and bishop of our souls. How can we possibly have energy to worry about other people, when the time will come to give our own accounting? Paul quotes a conflation of Isaiah 49:18 and 45:23 to make the point that none is exempt from this divine deposition. Note how this call to account is true for all people, Christian and non. The only difference is that the Christian has a defense attorney who, when all the charges have been presented and proven, nevertheless offers to take the sentence meted out to the offender upon himself, allowing the sinner to go free. This should make us all tremble. Our only goal in this life should be to not grieve the Holy Spirit by making things more difficult for others than they already are. God is pulling for others to succeed; we should too.

Do not, for food, destroy God's people

But resolve this instead, not to put a stumbling block or hindrance in the way of a brother.

14 I know and am persuaded in *the* Lord Jesus that nothing *is* unclean in itself,

but to one who considers something unclean, to that one *it is* unclean.

15 If your brother is being injured because of your food, you are no longer walking in love.

Do not by your food destroy one for whom Anointed died.

16 Don't let your good be spoken of as evil. 17 For God's kingdom is not eating and drinking, but justfulness and peace and joy in *the* holy spirit.

18 Whoever serves the Anointed in this *is* pleasing to God and approved by all.

19 So then, let us strive for the *things* of peace and of upbuilding one another.

20 Do not, for the sake of food, destroy God's work.

All things *are* indeed clean,

but *it is* wrong for anyone to eat with offense *to others*.

21 It *is* noble not to eat meat or drink wine or *do anything* in which your brother is offended.

22 *The* conviction you have, keep to yourself before God.

Blessed *is* the one who does not condemn himself in what he approves.

23 But whoever doubts is condemned if he eats, because *it is* not from faith.

Everything not from faith is sin.

VV. 13B–14

We would do well today to remember Paul's conclusion on this matter. Christians have made a fetish of deciding what God does and does not like. Whether it's alcohol, cigars, bathing suits for women, television, movies, dancing, clothes, hats, or means of conveyance, there's a Christian group out there who feel they've heard from the Lord once and for all about what they and others should do in these matters. Paul argues that we are to make up our own minds about these things, and then stick to what we feel is right for us. It's true that cigars stink and too much alcohol can hurt you. Personally, I agree with Newton Minow who said that if you watch American programming, you will witness "a vast wasteland."[3] There's good and bad in just about everything, and it's up to us to decide how much we can tolerate.

V. 15

Back to *food*, but the principle is readily applied to alcohol consumption. Whereas most Christians have no trouble with food, it's common for dedicated Christians to condemn the drinking of alcohol. Some say, falsely, that it's prohibited in the Bible. Others point out, rightly, that alcohol abuse can cause such pain that sometimes it's better to do without. The temptation to drink can ruin an event for a genuine alcoholic, and care must be taken to make sure that we neither tempt them with failure nor make light of the struggle they face. If it's going to be a problem for a brother, then our abstinence is a sign of our regard for our Lord and them.

V. 16

The converse is also true. If something really is good, we shouldn't let others belittle it and make Christianity an ascetic religion. One of the ministries of Christians is to remove some of the taboos about creation that have been instituted in pagan religions. In Christ we have immense freedom, and to portray that freedom as worship can go far in freeing others from superstition. When there's a legitimate danger to others because of our freedom we should restrain ourselves in deference to them. When they're just being religious and saying that gifts from God cannot be enjoyed, then we would be remiss to give heed to their objections. It's a matter of deciding if they have a point, or if they're just being religious prigs.

3. Speech to National Association of Broadcasters, May 9, 1961.

V. 17

God really doesn't care about what we eat and drink apart from how those activities affect our health. Jesus made the point, and we should move on from these picayunish details to the weightier matters of being spiritual people who have inner peace and joy. Think about how many people act like crabs because they don't have any genuine emancipation in their hearts. The best witness a Christian can have is to be happy and contented. It's been said that most people live with guilt about the past, boredom with the present, and anxiety about the future. Jesus solves all those problems, by forgiving our sins, guiding us into fruitful labors each day, and assuring us that tomorrow is in his hands. When we make Jesus our king, we perceive the existence of a kingdom where we can afford to feel better because things, in fact, are better.

V. 18

It's funny how when we obey God, things go better with other people as well. People may chirp about your religion and take pot shots at your conservatism, but the hope is that deep down they may in fact respect you and wish for what you have. It's not hard to please God: we just have to stop running from him, accept forgiveness and power from his son, and do what he says on a daily basis—one day at a time. Religion is hard; Christianity is easy.

V. 19

Strive. That sounds like work, and I just said it was easy. Well, it is work, but it's work for which we are suited. What does man want, Freud asks, but to work and to love? God suits our tasks to our nature, which is all anybody can ask.

VV. 20–21

Can we stop talking about food? Apparently not. Fundamentalists need to take note: here food stands for any shibboleth we raise as a measure of the piety of other Christians that is outside of the commands of our Lord himself. Paul is careful to say when he's giving his own opinion, and we should too. We cannot tolerate, in these lax times, people who call themselves

Christian yet who abrogate basic laws of moral behavior. That's not what Paul's talking about. He's talking about *adiaphora*, things indifferent, matters that are debatable.

Wine. Alcohol is still an issue, but again, it's a matter of the genuine harm it can bring, not simply that some people don't like it. There are annotated copies of the Scriptures in circulation today that argue that God does not condone the drinking of fermented beverages, and that all positive references in the Bible are to non-fermented drinks. Such commentaries make Christians look like bad scholars as well as party-poopers, and they should be ignored. The guideline is this: is there the possibility of actual harm, or is it simply somebody's opinion?

V. 22

We would have less schism in the church if people followed Paul's admonition and kept opinions about trivialities to themselves. It is possible to arouse God's ire and grieve the Holy Spirit by having opinions that God does not have. When we inject our likes and dislikes into the life of the church, we throw gas on the fire of contention. Do not elevate personal affinities to the level of doctrine. When we do, we give other Christians the right to take leave and non-Christians the right to discount the claims of Christ.

V. 23

The role of *sin* in the life of the converted believer is confusing. On the one hand, our sins have been covered, one and all, by the blood of Christ on the Cross. They will never be brought up, because in God's mind, they do not exist. On the other hand, sin that is *persisted in* still has the power to destroy because it will interfere with the life of the Spirit in us, and we will remain powerless and fruitless until it's repented of. Sin is no longer a problem in a primary sense, but sins are still a problem in a secondary sense, in that they enervate the Spirit.

Faith here means all that we receive from the risen Christ by way of guidance. If we do things that Jesus doesn't tell us to do, it's the same as if we do things he tells us to not do. Obedience involves not only doing the good and avoiding the bad, but it also involves realizing that there is much that is neither good nor bad and is therefore the province of our personal choice. By having doubts about the freedoms we have in Christ, we become neurotic and open Christ up to ridicule.

Chapter 15

PRÉCIS

This is the second half of the final A section. Paul entreats these strange bedfellows to not only tolerate each other, but to actively embrace one another. He reminds them that they are but one congregation in a much larger church, which extends from one end of the known world to the other. If the larger church lives in unity, so can they. He stresses that the unifying principle of the church is that of authority—Christ's authority, and by delegation, Paul's.

The strong should bear with the weak

15 We the strong ought to bear with the weaknesses of the weak,
and not to please ourselves.
2 Each of us should please the neighbor for good, toward upbuilding.
3 For the Anointed did not please himself,
but as it is written: "The insults of those who insulted you fell on me."
4 For whatever was written before
for our instruction was written,
so that by perseverance
and by the encouragement of the scriptures
we may have hope.
5 The God of perseverance and encouragement
may he enable you
to agree with one another,
according to Anointed Jesus,

6 so together in one voice
you may glorify
the God and Father of our Lord Jesus Anointed.

V. 1

This section begins with a continuation of the thought in the final verses of chapter 14. What Paul's saying is that people who are *weak* in faith, who have doubts as to what constitutes right behavior, should not only be tolerated, but encouraged. God is God not only of the intelligent, wise, and astute, but he is also God of the simple, the silly, and the confused. What's clear to us is not always clear to others, and that's part of the penalty when we ourselves are perspicacious.

VV. 2–3

Sometimes it's hard to find something to commend in others, but we all stand in need of affirmation. There is a sacramental quality to Christian leadership whereby the leader, who by definition has greater knowledge and perception, has to suffer so that others might be edified. It can be argued that the ability to separate duty and personal feelings is what makes men better candidates for church leadership.[1] Aspiration to leadership is not about rights or abilities, but rather about being granted a license to suffer.[2] Sometimes it is the priest himself who is the sacrifice, along the lines of Isaac. To consistently put others first and to seek their welfare above one's own comfort requires a certain focus and dedication to principle—something that often competes with concern for interpersonal relationships. Paul quotes Psalm 69:9b to illustrate that this principle of vicarious suffering starts with Christ and can therefore be expected of those who claim to follow him, especially those in leadership.

V. 4

Paul lays out the purpose of the Scriptures in one sentence. They were written to teach us what is to happen and why. Life is difficult, especially for the person who tries to lead a principled life. When trials come, as they

1. 1 Tim 2:12.
2. Jas 3:1.

must, we must be able to interpret them in the proper light, that instead of despairing, we might find encouragement. *Hope* of better things or ultimate redemption can come only when we see the big picture.

VV. 5–6

Not only do we draw benefit from the Scriptures as individuals, but also as a body. When the many draw upon the same source for inspiration and direction, the result is agreement. The NIV translates *homothymadon* as *one heart*; Bailey's translation gives *together*. The NIV interpolation may be justified, for it captures the sense that the Gospel generates community in a unique way. Right doctrine brings people together and results in worship.

Welcome one another, Jews and Gentiles, as Anointed welcomed you

7 Therefore welcome one another, as the Anointed also welcomed you, for God's glory.

8 For I say that Anointed became a servant of *the* circumcised on behalf of God's truthfulness, in order to confirm the promises to the fathers,

9 and that the Gentiles may glorify God for mercy, as it is written:

"For this I will praise you among *the* Gentiles, and to your name sing praise."

10 And again it says: "Rejoice, you Gentiles, with his people."

11 And again: "Praise the Lord, all you Gentiles, and let all the peoples praise him."

12 And again Isaiah says: "There will be the offshoot of Jesse, he who will rise up to rule *the*

Gentiles, in him *the* Gentiles will hope."

13 May the God of hope fill you with all joy and peace in believing, so that you may abound in hope through *the* holy spirit's power.

V. 7

At every opportunity, Paul reverts to his primary argument that Jews and Gentiles have reason to not only get along with one another, but to actively embrace each other as fellow Christians. When we do what we would otherwise not do simply on the basis of revelation, we justify God's plan and cause him to be praised. Like the evident chiasmus, the story starts with the Jews, comes to include Gentiles, and concludes, in verse 10, with the two united in worship.

VV. 8–12

Here is a two-part assertion with a single conclusion. God's plan of redemption involves the Jews, for it honors the promises made to the patriarchs. God has said he calls and elects those who conform to the patriarchs' pattern of faith and behavior. This call is valid and true without regard to the response of their descendants. That transitory unfaithfulness prevails among many Jews has resulted in the promise being broadened to include Gentiles. What applies to the first group now applies to the both, which is a gesture of profound mercy. Paul quotes Psalm 18:49, where the NIV substitutes *nations* for *Gentiles*. They are the same concept to any Jew. He also quotes Deuteronomy 32:43, which uses the same NIV substitution. A third quote from Psalm 117:1 matches almost verbatim. Finally, he gives a rough quote of Isaiah 11:10, followed by a snippet of Isaiah 42:4b. This last fragment was also paraphrased by Matthew in 12:21, where *Law* becomes *name*, and *islands* becomes *nations*. We can guess that the Septuagint or other versions of the Old Testament made these substitutions, which in no way changes the thrust of the passages. The word *islands* refers to the islands of the eastern Mediterranean where non-Jewish peoples resided, hence *Gentiles* for Paul. No doubt Paul occupied himself during his three years in Arabia rereading the Hebrew Scriptures for references to the coming Messiah, and these are the passages that stuck in his mind. Again, verse 10 constitutes the conclusion of the chiasmus, where Gentiles rejoice with *his people*, the Jews.

V. 13

The theme is of the *hope* spoken of by Isaiah, so Paul repeats the concept as being an actual fulfillment of an ancient prophecy. When we are filled with the Spirit of Jesus, there are tangible benefits. Because he solves our two major problems in life, guilt and powerlessness, we will have *joy and peace*. What is joy, what is peace, beyond a certitude that we are safe and well taken care of? Christianity works.

Confidence in the Romans, Paul's plans and request for prayer, benedictions, greetings[53]

Confidence in the Romans, Paul's ministry and plans, request for prayer

14 Confident am I, my brothers,
  even I myself,
    about you,
  that even yourselves,

full are you of goodness, filled with all knowledge, and able to instruct one another.

15 Rather boldly have I written to you on some points, as reminding you,

because of the grace given me by God

16 for me to be Anointed Jesus' minister to the Gentiles,

ministering God's good news,

so that the offering of the Gentiles may be acceptable, made holy in *the* holy spirit.

17 I have, then, reason for boasting in Anointed Jesus in things pertaining to God.

18 To be sure I will not dare to speak of anything except what
Anointed has accomplished through me toward obedience of *the*
Gentiles, by word and deed, 19 by power of signs and wonders, by
power of spirit,

for me, from Jerusalem and round about as far as Illyricum,

to complete the good news,

the Anointed's.

20 In this way endeavoring to preach the good news,

not where Anointed has been named, so that I do not build on another's foundation,

21 but as it is written: "Those who were not told of him will see, and those who have not heard will understand."

22 That is why **I have been unable for so long**

to come to you.

23 But now, no further place having in these regions, and **a longing having**

to come to you

for many years,

24 as I go to Spain, I hope on my journey to see you, and by you to be sent on my way there,

after I have enjoyed you for a while.

25 But now I am going to Jerusalem, serving the holy *ones*.

26 For Macedonia and Achaia were pleased to make some contribution for the poor among the holy *ones* at Jerusalem.[54]

27 They were pleased, and indeed they are their debtors,
for if the Gentiles have shared in their spiritual *blessings*,
they ought also to serve them in material *blessings*.
28 So when I have completed this, and have sealed to them this fruit,
I will set out by way of you to Spain.

[53] 15:14—16:23 ABCDCBA. The fourth of five divisions of this letter. Parallel with 1:8–17.

[54] 15:26 Apparently Galatia failed to participate. See 1 Cor 16:1–4; Gal 2:10; 2 Cor 8:1–6; 9:1–2.

VV. 14–15

Paul gets personal. What he has been discussing in the abstract he now applies to his audience in Rome. Having stated the ideal, he's now saying that theory has become reality in and among themselves. Note how he associates *goodness*, *knowledge*, and the ability to *instruct*. Christianity is not some supernatural sensation, it is a logical system based on facts of history that can be learned, verified, and put into practice. What is the proof that it's true? That bad men are made good. He now realizes that he's been rather dogmatic and forceful on a variety of subjects, mostly related to the Jew/Gentile issue. Now that he's finishing up, he wants to modify his strident tone somewhat. Regardless of how he appeared, he wrote this way because of God's grace, the Spirit of Jesus in him, which was imparted to him in order to accomplish a very specific task, which was to preach the Gospel to the Gentile world. They, too, are to become a living sacrifice, along with the Jews, acceptable to God on an even basis with their Hebrew brothers. Both Jew and Gentile rely upon the indwelling Holy Spirit to live lives pleasing to God, and as such they are co-equal.

V. 16

Ministering or *priestly duty* (NIV). This word comes from the root *hiereus* which is translated as priest. Paul argues that what he's doing is no less a priestly office than the Levitical priesthood who offered animal sacrifices as a part of worship. Instead of offering animals that are to be killed, Paul offers the majority of humanity, the Gentile world, as a living sacrifice that will glorify God through their purified worship and godly behavior. In the church, a priest is not merely a pastor. The pastor takes his title from the barnyard; he is to shepherd people as one does animals—to feed and control them. The priest on the other hand, takes his title from the history of God's people, the Israelites. He is to act as an intermediary between God and man, offering pastoral guidance to be sure, but also administering the sacraments of baptism and the Lord's Supper. These two sacraments represent the two main components in God's plan of redemption: Christ's death on the Cross for our justification, and his ongoing life as the empowering Lord. These sacraments are given to us by Jesus as ceremonies through which the believer is taken back in time, variously to the Cross or the Last Supper, to find themselves included in those events no less than the disciples. They are for our edification, and Christian ministers who fail to understand or perform them are offering only a partial and imperfect ministry to their flocks. We need to be identified with Christ's death on the cross, and the act of immersion conveys this—we are buried with Christ. We need to be refilled with the Holy Spirit on at least a weekly basis; when we kneel at the communion rail, we are beseeching him to nourish his Spirit in us, that he might minister to and through us. We do not receive Christ once and for all; We don't say the sinner's prayer just once, those who worship according to the 1928 *Book of Common Prayer* say it weekly in the "Prayer of Humble Access" and the "Confession of Sin." People who receive proper ministry become a living sacrifice to God and bear fruit to his glory. As such, Paul has become priest to the Gentiles, not just a pastor.

VV. 17, 20

Paul boasts of his ministry, something Martin Luther fully understood.[3] Paul is excited about what he's doing. When you enjoy your work, it's not a job. He chose to become a minister to the Gentiles, I suppose, for two reasons. First of all, nobody else wanted to do it. Tradition has it that Thomas traveled abroad with the Gospel, and others may have as well. We know Philip went to what was Philistine territory. Peter and John went to Samaria and turned right around. None, however, documented their work to the extent Paul did, nor did they refine their theology to justify their focus on ministry to non-Jews. The Letter to the Romans to this point has been an exposé of Paul's understanding of the mystery of God: that Jew and Gentile

3. Martin writes, "Every minister should make much of his calling and impress upon others the fact that he has been delegated by God to preach the Gospel. As the ambassador of a government is honored for his office and not for his private person, so the minister of Christ should exalt his office in order to gain authority among men. This is not vainglory, but needful glorying." Luther, *Commentary*, 10.

should be reconciled to God and each other by Jesus Christ. Secondly, the Gentiles were an easier audience than the Jews. Wherever Paul went, he would start talking in the synagogues, but when that proved controversial, he would then take up with the Gentiles in the area. It's still true that it's easier to persuade somebody who's never heard the Gospel at all than somebody who's heard part or a distorted version of it, and therefore think they know all truth. Another's foundation may be good, but then again, it may not be. Paul was seeking a blank slate as his audience, wisely.

VV. 18–19.

Obedience or *obey* (NIV). This is an outdated concept that we need to resurrect. Note that Paul uses every means at his disposal: *word and deed, signs and wonders*, and *power of spirit*, in order to lead Gentiles to obey God. How did we ever get it so wrong regarding what God's looking for, that we might say he creates some for eternal felicity and some for eternal damnation by fiat? Both Luther and Calvin got this wrong, saying we can't inquire into God's counsels for why he chooses some and not others.[4] No. God wants a response, and it's within reach. His directive is that we should obey him, that we should cede our will and regard Jesus as Lord. It's a question of authority, purely and simply. Our response is negative; we stop running and shut up. The problem with the liberal church today is that they do not *fully* (NIV) proclaim the Gospel. There are two halves, as Paul points out. To preach only the first half, what God has done for us in Christ's death, is to dishonor Jesus as Lord and do your audience a huge disservice. So, we've been forgiven, do we continue to wallow in the same filth, only to need more forgiveness? Paul's already addressed this point. No. There's a second half to the Gospel: what God's looking for by way of response. We don't do it; Christ does it in us. But if we refuse to let him do so, we get in spiritual trouble.[5]

VV. 21–22

Paul quotes Isaiah 52:15b. Gentile peoples were ignorant of special revelation, and the news of a Messiah would be a completely novel concept. Just because they've never heard of him doesn't mean that he's not of interest

4. Luther, *Commentary*, 16; Calvin, *Institutes*, 922.

5. "God nowhere holds a person responsible for having the heredity of sin and does not condemn anyone because of it. Condemnation comes when I realize that Jesus Christ came to deliver me from this heredity of sin, and yet I refuse to let Him do so. From that moment I begin to get the seal of damnation." Chambers, *My Utmost*, October 5.

to them. It's the job of the evangelist to find out what a culture says about the big questions: life, death, morals, and purpose, and to show how Jesus makes sense of them all. As Isaiah says, when Jesus died on the cross, he justified all of humanity. Paul's been delayed in coming to Rome because he's so busy bringing the Gospel to the Gentiles he meets along the way. He was *needs* driven. When necessary, he tarried to establish a healthy congregation that could then take care of itself until his return. He knew that follow-up and discipleship were necessary so that sudden enthusiasm could be transformed into lasting faith.

VV. 23–24

Uh oh, Paul's making plans. Yes, he'll get to Rome, but not in the way he thinks. He says that he's completed his church planting in *these regions*, meaning around Corinth, where he probably was when he wrote this letter. Earlier he had been prevented from entering Asia proper and instead had a vision of a Macedonian man asking he go there. Thus, his ministry has been limited to Greece and what we call Asia Minor; Italy and Rome still lay to the west. Being an ambitious man, he wants to go farther west still, to Spain, after he visits Rome. There is absolutely no evidence Paul ever made it to Spain, in fact we know that he was arrested in Jerusalem and held in custody of some sort in Rome until his execution. This fact has not discouraged the Chamber of Commerce in parts of Spain from seizing upon this verse and verse 28 in claiming he escaped from prison and the executioner to in fact make it to their country.[6]

VV. 25–28

The last part of Paul's plan that is accurate is that he's going to go to Jerusalem to deliver the offering gathered for their relief. Even though Paul contended with the Jerusalem saints from time to time, he always recognized their primacy in terms of their coming to faith in Christ before him, and his debt to them by persecuting them before his conversion. He often points out that spiritual revelation has a value that can and should be expressed in financial terms. We have material needs, and we have spiritual needs. Living in a world of scarcity, we should be sure both are tended to. This takes money. He was no ascetic or Gnostic, saying that the spiritual is good and the material bad. Material wealth is not an end in itself, but a means to

6. See Meinardus, "Paul's Missionary Journey."

an end that God sanctifies. He's already said that revelation starts with the Jewish people, and Gentiles are in their debt, regardless of how the Jews of his day acted. Paul viewed his diligence in keeping his promise to the impoverished in Jerusalem as a demonstration of his trustworthiness in other matters. He mentions Spain again; he would lose his freedom before this could become a reality.

> 29 I know that in coming to you, in fullness of Anointed's blessing I will come.
>
> 30 I urge you, by our Lord Jesus Anointed and by the love of the spirit,
> to struggle with me by prayers for me to God,
> 31 that I may be delivered from the disobedient in Judea,
> and *that* my service for Jerusalem may be acceptable to the holy *ones*,
> 32 so that with joy coming to you by *the* will of God, I may be refreshed together with you.
>
> **Peace benediction**
>
> 33 The God of peace *be* with all of you. Amen.

V. 29

Paul wants the Roman congregation to know that when he comes, he will do so in keeping with the Lord's will. He is not coming to correct or admonish them, but to bring encouragement and blessing from the living Lord.

VV. 30–33

Paul has a pretty good idea that there is going to be trouble in Judea when he goes there to drop off his offering to the Saints. He terms his ministry there a struggle, in which he will be in conflict with *unbelievers* (NIV) or the *disobedient*. This word has the same root as our *apathetic*. When there is disagreement on fundamentals, such as God and his will for his creation, there will always be conflict. We often define Christians as peaceful, loving people who do all they can to avoid conflict. This is fine in trivial matters, but Paul realizes that he's provoked the Jewish authorities in Jerusalem by his ministry, and a final conflict is looming. There will be prophecy to this effect recorded in the Acts of the Apostles, but Paul insists on going there anyway.[7] By avoiding conflict early on, we often make the ultimate struggle worse. Paul may have hoped that by drawing the ire of the religious

7. Acts 20:23; 21:11.

authorities in Jerusalem, he might grant some peace to the Saints who still live and minister in the city. He was first and foremost a fighter, and he was actively attracted to the contest. He appealed to Caesar when he didn't have to, but in doing so he brought greater attention to the claims of Christ. We need more men like Paul in the church today.

Paul's desire that he go to Rome in joy for refreshment was not to be. He came in chains, and according to tradition, he was kept in custody until his execution. In spite of his awareness of the precariousness of his position, his focus is on God as a God of peace. Peace is not the absence of conflict, but the triumph of rectitude.

Chapter 16

PRÉCIS

The Bible is in a very real sense a book of names. God traces human history using names and places to show that these people really lived, and their lives were touched by God. Paul, being a reader of the Bible, also employs names to place his ministry in the context of real people who were experiencing the touch of God in their own day. We can only guess who were Jews and who were Gentiles, but we know that their problems served as call and inspiration for Paul to lay forth the most complete and comprehensive account of theology, both theoretical and practical, in the whole of the New Testament.

Commendation of the letter carrier

16 I commend to you Phoebe our sister, who is a **deacon** of the church at Cenchreae,[55]

2 that you may welcome her in *the* Lord
in a manner worthy of the holy *ones*,
and help her in whatever from you she may need,
for she has been a **patron** to many and to me as well.

[55] 16:1 *Cenchreae.* The eastern port of Corinth. Paul sent this letter from Corinth within AD 51–58.

VV. 1–2

Having already given a benediction and said *Amen*, Paul realizes he must do some housekeeping before ending his letter. Ever the diplomat, he brings to mind all his connections to the Roman congregation. The first of these is Phoebe, who's a *deacon* or *servant* (NIV) in the church at Cenchreae, where Paul may have been when writing this letter. Apparently she was making plans to go to Rome, and Paul wanted to vouch for her ministry. The New Testament makes a case for the office of deacon being distinct and separate from that of presbyter or overseer, and whenever the term deacon is used formally, it's assumed to refer to males.[1] Paul uses the term deacon here, and also for himself and others in a manner that the NIV translates as *servant*, *minister*, or *attendant*. Of the 29 times this word was used in the New Testament, only three times is it translated in the NIV as *deacon* or *deacons*. Women played a significant role in ministering to the needs of Jesus, the disciples, and other Christian ministers. The use of the word deacon in this case should not be taken to mean that the ordained office of deacon was open to women. Even in ancient times, the Enemy has sought to sexualize and feminize worship in order to make it more attractive to the carnal and craven.

Greetings to those in Rome[56]

3 Greet Prisca[57] and Aquila, my fellow workers in Anointed Jesus, 4
who risked their necks for my life, to whom not only I give thanks but
also **all the churches of the Gentiles**;

5 *greet* also the church in their house.

Greet Epaenetus, my beloved, who is *the* first fruit of Asia to Anointed.

6 Greet Mary, who has worked hard for you.

7 Greet Andronicus and Junia,[58] my kin and my fellow prisoners, who are prominent among

the apostles, and who were before me **in Anointed.**

8 Greet Ampliatus, my beloved **in *the* Lord.**

9 Greet Urbanus, our fellow worker **in Anointed**, and Stachys, my beloved.

10 Greet Apelles, approved **in Anointed.**

Greet those of the *household* of Aristobulus.

11 Greet Herodion, my kinsman.

Greet those of the *household* of Narcissus who are **in *the* Lord.**

12 Greet Tryphaena and Tryphosa, hard workers **in *the* Lord.**

Greet Persis, the beloved, who has worked hard **in *the* Lord.**

13 Greet Rufus, the chosen **in *the* Lord**, and his mother and mine.

14 Greet Asyncritus, Phlegon, Hermes, Patrobas, Hermas, and the brothers with them.

1. Acts 6:3; 1 Tim 3:8.

15 Greet Philologus and Julia, Nereus and his sister, and Olympas, and all the holy *ones* with them.

16 Greet one another with a holy kiss.

Greeting you are **all the churches of the Anointed.**

[56] 16:3–16 ABCDCBA. The center of this division. These 18 greetings are arranged in 7 groups.

[57] 16:3 *Prisca.* "Priscilla" in Acts. Acts 18:1–3 records that when Paul first came to Corinth on his second missionary journey he stayed and made tents with Priscilla and Aquila, who had recently been expelled with the Jews from Rome. Acts 18:18–19 says that they accompanied Paul when he left Corinth about 18 months later, and went with him to Ephesus, where Paul left them. When Paul returned to Ephesus on his third missionary journey, 1 Cor 16:19 indicates they were still there. Now they are evidently back in Rome. 2 Tim 4:19, which indicates it was written from Rome, places them back in or near Ephesus. The Jews were expelled from Rome by the emperor Claudius about 49, because of "disturbances at the instigation of Chrestus" (Suetonius, *Claudius* 25.4). When Nero became emperor in 54, he allowed the Jews to return.

[58] 16:7 This could be either "Junia," a common feminine name that occurs more than 250 times in Greek and Latin inscriptions found in Rome alone, or an hypothetical abbreviation, Junias, that has never been found in inscriptions, for Junianus, a masculine name. See Omanson's article in *Bible Review* (December 1998, pages 40–41). Some translations prefer the masculine name because Paul refers to the person as an "apostle."

VV. 3–4

Priscilla and Aquila were Jews who joined Paul in tentmaking as a trade. He met them in Corinth after they had been expelled from Rome by imperial edict on account of their religion. Perhaps they had been allowed back into Rome and would be visiting the congregation there. They apparently had a congregation already meeting in their own home. House churches were fine in their day, and in oppressive countries they are no doubt the only way the church can operate. Churches need to recover many of the ministries taken away from them by government, such as education, health care, charity, and hospitality. For these activities, church buildings are necessary. We should never look down on those facilities built and consecrated for holy purposes.

VV. 5–16

Paul goes on to urge greetings for those he knows to already be in Rome and in contact with the congregation he's writing to. By my count, these are all gentiles with the exception of those he refers to as *kin* or *relatives* (NIV).

Elizabeth and Mary were referred to as *relative*,[2] yet were clearly not closely related to each other beyond being fellow Jews, for Mary and Joseph were of the tribe of Judah, and Zechariah and Elizabeth were both of the tribe of Levi. Like Luke, Paul uses the term *relative* as a euphemism for fellow Jew. He's trying to tamp down the racial and religious distinctions already so prevalent in a heterogeneous congregation such as in Rome. I put the count at five Jews and at least twenty-one Gentiles. However, it's impossible to definitively judge ethnicity by name, for many Jews adopted Latin names.

In Christ (NIV) or *in the Lord*. Here Paul does not use the term in a technically precise manner as he does when discussing soteriology, where we are placed *in Christ* by the Cross. Here he's using it loosely to refer to being a Christian, having Christ's approval, working for Jesus, or elect in keeping with God's plan of redemption. He uses the descriptor as a compliment, to commend people for their faithfulness to the risen Lord. As a true ambassador, he's establishing a link between the churches he has founded and this Roman congregation founded by others.

Warning, rejoicing for those in Rome

17 I urge you, brothers, to watch out for those who cause divisions and temptations contrary to the teaching that you learned, and avoid them.

18 For such do not serve our Lord Anointed, but their own stomach, and by smooth talk and praises they deceive the hearts of the unwary.

19 Your obedience[59] is known to all,

over you, therefore, I rejoice;

but I want you to be wise to the good, and innocent to the evil.

20 The God of peace will crush the Adversary under your feet quickly.

Grace benediction

The grace of our Lord Jesus *be* with you.

[59] 16:19 *Obedience*. A fulfillment of 1:5 and 16:26.

VV. 17–19

No sooner does Paul speak of spiritual felicity that crosses all boundaries than he warns of threats that lurk within the body. A wise man said, no doubt a clergyman, "The devil doesn't oppose churches, he joins them." Paul's making clear reference to the Judaizers, for he mentions *divisions and obstacles* (NIV) or *divisions and temptations*. The strategy of the "circumcision group"

2. Luke 1:36.

was invariable: they would resurrect the notion of the primacy of Jews over Gentiles based upon the spiritual heritage of the former. They would point to the disgusting moral practices of pagans and use that as an excuse to reintroduce Mosaic Law as a standard for Christian behavior. They would not stop at the moral content of the Law but would reimpose the sacramental aspects as well—notably circumcision and dietary restrictions. Paul has already beaten this horse to death, but he is convinced that this threat outweighs any other. He goes so far as to warn that such people should not even be associated with. Sometimes in our efforts to be inclusive and fair we invite elements into the life of the congregation who resist ministry, add nothing, and take away a great deal. Sometimes we cannot afford the benefit of fellowship with certain people. They may be charming, but pernicious in their effect on the body. Wisdom involves careful parsing of people and their motives. As Rabbi Ed Friedman said, "Kick the trouble-makers out."[3]

V. 20

Note how a God of peace crushes all opposition. It's only after Satan is crushed that we will experience peace. We don't do it; God does it, but he uses our feet. We are instruments wielding his power. Satan's tied to a chain, but if you go within the radius of the chain, you can be sure you'll be bitten as by a vicious dog.[4] The solution to this and every problem is *Grace*: Jesus living in us and granting us his power to reassert his hegemony over a lost and rebellious world. When we're under authority, we have authority; it's derivative. The liberal church antagonizes the Holy Spirit, then wonders why it has no power. The common refrain of those who heard Jesus was that he spoke "with authority."[5]

> **Greetings from those with Paul**
>
> 21 Greeting you is Timothy, my fellow worker, and Lucius and Jason and Sosipater, my kinsmen.
> 22 Greeting you am I, Tertius, the writer of this letter, in *the* Lord.
> 23 Greeting you is Gaius,[60] the host to me and to the whole church.
> Greeting you is Erastus, the city treasurer, and Quartus, the brother. [24]
>
> [60] 16:23 *Gaius* of Corinth was one of the few in Corinth baptized by Paul (1 Cor 1:14).

3. Comment made while addressing the clergy of the Episcopal Diocese of Colorado.
4. Rev 20:1–2.
5. Matt 7:29; Mark 1:22; Luke 4:32.

VV. 21–24

Greetings from Paul's end follow. He's in the company of an extended congregation, which seems to be of some stature. His host can afford to have not only Timothy and Paul come and stay, but other itinerant ministers of the Gospel as well. They also have a high city official in their midst—must be Episcopalians.

Blessing, summary of the good news, doxology[61]

25 Now to him who is able to strengthen you
according to my good news and Jesus Anointed's message,
according to *the* revelation of *the* mystery from times eternal kept secret
26 but now disclosed,
and through *the* prophetic scriptures,
according to *the* command of the eternal God,
for obedience of faithfulness into all nations,[62]
made known,
27 to *the* only wise God,
through Jesus Anointed,
to whom the **glory** into the ages. Amen.

[61] 16:25–27 The last of five divisions of this letter. The only Pauline letter closing that names and summarizes the good news. Parallel with 1:1–7, the only Pauline letter opening that names and summarizes the good news. The NA27 Greek text puts verses 25–27 in brackets because of divided manuscript support.

[62] 16:26 *For obedience of faithfulness into all nations* (see 1:5), a summary of the theme of this letter and a fulfillment of Gen 22:18. *All nations*, see Gal 3:8, Mark 13:10, Mat 28:19, Luke 24:47, and 2 Tim 4:17

VV. 25–27

The letter concludes with a hymn of praise in the form of a chiasmus. Paul's last word is not to his human audience, but to the Lord, who is the beginning and end of all consciousness for the believer. It is God who restores people to their right mind and behavior by his Gospel. Before the preaching of Christ, we are all on shaky ground. We don't know who we are or why we're here. In the absence of revelation, we degenerate into carnal indulgence and conflict with our fellow man. Even the special revelation granted to the Jew has done nothing but exacerbate the rivalries and jealousies of the nations. It is only with the full Gospel of Jew and Gentile equal before

God—equal in guilt and equal in redemption—that mankind is reconciled first to God, then to each other. In the story of Jesus Christ, all that was confusing and contradictory about the human condition has been put in its proper place and now makes sense. There is a parsimony and an elegance to God's plan of redemption. He did nothing that was unnecessary, and he did it as soon as his creation could sustain it. Paul sees himself as standing on a great divide, for in his conclusion in verse 26c, he says all is *now* done by *the command of the eternal God*. The news is not really new, for it was predicted and outlined in the writings of the Old Testament, which Paul has repeatedly cited throughout this letter. What was limited to the Jew is now the rightful possession of all nations. It is a Gospel where belief and obedience are synonymous; if it's true, then it's worth acting upon. Glory is accorded to those who take up the welfare of others, even at cost to themselves. God has revealed himself as a loving father who takes both the guilt and frailty of his children and puts them on his son, so that his son might have a chaste, spotless, and obedient bride, his Church. Amen. So be it.

Glossary of Soteriological Terms

Abide. To abide is to stay where one has been put. As of Good Friday, all have been put in Christ forensically. We are to stay there and take advantage of being considered sinless.

Atonement. Atonement is the result of the Cross from God's perspective. Humanity stands cleansed from sins and has the potential to escape from having a Sin nature. We can thus be filled with the Holy Spirit.

Baptism. One of the two dominical sacraments, baptism signifies our one-time justification and how we embark on the Christian journey. As Jesus' sacrifice on the Cross is perfect and need not be repeated, so our baptism is a one-time event not needing repetition. In the case of infants, this is a celebration of our justification which was accomplished by father and son without our knowledge, consent, or participation (Gen 15:17). As such, it should be followed with confirmation at the age of majority. In the case of adults, it is also an identification with the death of Christ in that we, too, die to self-interest and are raised to a new life of obedience. In both cases, baptism proclaims we in Christ legally. The sacrament transports us back in time and place to the Cross, showing we were involved.

Blaspheming the Holy Spirit. This is the one unforgivable sin. There are two aspects to this sin. First of all, it means calling the perfect ministry of the Holy Spirit wrong or irrelevant, thereby grieving him and driving him from our hearts. He will leave if we ask (Luke 8:37). Secondly, it means disobeying God's revealed Word, the Bible, which was authored by the Holy Spirit (Mark 3:29).

Call. God, in his permissive will, has called all humanity to participate in his perfect plan of redemption for a lost and rebellious humanity. This call, however, is not heard by all, but only by those who are disposed to obey what they hear. The call, therefore, is both general and particular. It is the work of the Holy Spirit, who "is the Deity in proceeding power who applies the Atonement to our experience."[1] God seeks co-laborers to host his Spirit and help redeem his fallen creation. We participated in our Fall, and we are therefore expected to participate in our redemption. All are called, both the "good and bad" (Matt 22:10). The call can be refused or neglected.

Conversion. Before a person can become regenerate, he has to come "to his senses" (Luke 15:17). That is, his thinking must become clear and his ability to reason restored. Only then can he engage in a moral transaction with God. When the mind is persuaded of the truth of God and his Gospel, a person is said to be converted. A reformation of worship allows conversion, and conversion allows regeneration.

Elect. This term is used by Jesus, Paul, and Peter. God, in his eternal counsels, has determined that those who are willing to accept both righteousness and power vicariously from Jesus are elect unto salvation, and are therefore not subject to the penalties of the final judgment. It is used to denote those who fulfill this new criterion, as opposed to those who rely upon race or obedience to the Law. This term is found in Scriptures addressed to a Gentile audience, in order to encourage them and show that they, no less than Jews, are acceptable to God.

Election. The eternal decree that a class or type of people are chosen for salvation and not reprobation. Specifically, that class or type who love God, and who are therefore willing to humble themselves and accept righteousness and power vicariously from Jesus. It does not refer to individuals per se, as the decree precedes human history. Synonymous with *choice*, *foreknowledge*.

Eucharist, Holy Communion. One of two Dominical sacraments, the eucharist relates to God's Grace, that is, Christ dwelling in us. Just as we are physically nourished by food and drink, the Spirit of Jesus in us requires repeated nutrition. This sacrament needs to be repeated as we need to be filled with the Spirit on an ongoing basis (Acts 13:9; 52). Jesus emphasizes that the elements are his body and blood, not those of animals as in Genesis 15 (Jer 34:18). The miracle of this celebration is that the elements of bread and wine effectually become the same loaf and cup as those consecrated by Jesus at the Last Supper, meaning the promises made to the disciples then are valid for disciples today. Holy

1. Chambers, *My Utmost*, April 8.

Communion transports us back in time and place to the Last Supper; we were there.

Foreknowledge. Foreknowledge is God's expectation that people of a "good heart" would hear of his plan of redemption and cooperate with it (Luke 8:15). This refers to a class or type of person, not individuals. These are people who love God (Rom 8:28).

Fruit. All people are called to reproduce divine faith in others. God has chosen to work with and through his children for the redemption of humanity. Fruitfulness becomes the new criterion according to which all people will be judged (Matt 25:31–46).

Glorification. God gives glory to all who cooperate with his plan of redemption when they die. God imparts Christ's glory to us as his brothers and sisters.

Glory. Glory accrues to all who willingly take on unmerited suffering in order to further the welfare of others. This describes the father, son and Holy Spirit altogether. As a grateful humanity we are to ascribe glory to God without reservation. God shares his glory with those who suffer to build up his kingdom.

Grace. Grace is God's decree and the reality that the Spirit of Jesus abides in those who obey him as Lord. These are those who cease running from God and who cede their will to that same Holy Spirit. Grace is Christ in us effectually.

Hardening. The process, mandated by God but initiated by man, whereby those who deliberately rebel against the ministry of the Holy Spirit are progressively deprived of spiritual discernment. Spiritual apostasy is followed by distorted mentation and then dissolute behavior. All are born with a conscience, which is a remnant of the Spirit we had in the Garden. This conscience, which is to lead us to God, becomes seared as with a hot iron in those who persist in sin in order to presage life without God (1 Tim 4:2). Hardening follows impenitence, not the other way around.

Justification. Justification is distinct from salvation (Rom 5:9–10; 10:9–10). God justifies all humanity without restriction by covering their sins with the blood of Christ his son. Justification is universal. On the Cross all the demands of the Law are fulfilled; all are in Christ legally. Justification is retroactive to men and women who lived before Good Friday. Jesus is the Savior of all.

Law. The Law is a manifestation of God's inherent moral rectitude, and it requires that those who would know God live in moral perfection. The Law cannot be obeyed. It is imperfectly expressed in the Mosaic Law delivered on Mount Sinai. It is fulfilled and rendered obsolete by Christ's perfect life and obedient death on the Cross.

Monergistic. This denotes an action, in this case by God, that is accomplished without reference to another entity, in this case, man. Standards for election, predestination to Christ-likeness, our justification, and our glorification are all monergistic actions on God's part.

Ordo Salutis. The order of salvation is the formal term for God's mechanism of salvation, or plan of redemption. Attempts to formulate an agreeable Ordo based on Romans 8:28–30 have historically foundered.

Pelagius. A British monk active in the fourth and fifth centuries who maintained that Adam's transgression affected him alone, and therefore others can obey God without the aid of the Holy Spirit. He was correctly anathematized by Councils at Carthage in 416 and 418 and Mileve in 416.

Predestination. God doesn't merely excuse, but actually reforms the spiritual, intellectual and physical aspects of those who participate in his redemptive plan. God saves in reality, not just in a forensic sense. The elect are predestined to be conformed to the likeness of Jesus, also described as being adopted into God's family. This reflects God's will that Christians be actually transformed into Christ-like people while they yet live. Never in Scripture does it refer to some sort of spiritual determinism following death.

Preterition. A term used to connote the withholding of grace from an individual. For Calvin, preterition was arbitrary, to show God's justice. Preterition is not arbitrary, but it occurs on account of an individual's determination to grieve the Holy Spirit through deliberate ignorance or disobedience while they live.

Promise. God makes promises to mankind through specific revelation that he will redeem a lost and sinful humanity. The promise was first manifested in the Abrahamic covenant established in Genesis 15; the smoking firepot and flaming torch represent the father and the son redeeming humanity sovereignly. Promise finds its fulfillment in the events of Good Friday and Pentecost. It refers to all that God has done for us.

Redemption. On the basis of his entry for February 1st, we join Oswald Chambers in defining redemption as we in Christ, with an emphasis on the human perspective. We are put in Christ's position of righteousness legally as of Good Friday. This is a universal truth for all humanity. See *Justification*.

Regeneration. When the Spirit of Jesus comes to dwell in a person, they are said to be regenerate. They are once again a three-part person, as in the Garden before the Fall. Regeneration is synonymous with baptism in the Holy Spirit, being born again, being filled with the Holy Spirit, etc. Those who obey Jesus as Lord are predestined to become regenerate.

Reprobation. The provision of punishment to all people who either ignore or actively rebel against God's perfect plan of salvation (Matt 21:44). It involves separation from God and suffering, and it seems to imply ongoing existence in Chronos. Reprobation is contrasted with the provision of glory to those who do in fact cooperate with that perfect plan.

Righteousness. Righteousness is moral rectitude, as held exclusively by God. It can be imputed to man as an ascription due to the Cross.

Salvation. Salvation is distinct from justification (Rom 5:9–10; 10:9–10). Those in whom Christ dwells are said to have their names written in the Book of Life; His life is in them (Rev 20:11–15). Because of this grace, they are able to do good to others, notably other Christians (Matt 25:31–46). Salvation is particular to the individual, and it requires they accept both righteousness and power vicariously from Jesus. Christ cannot dwell in those who grieve his Holy Spirit.

Sanctification. Sanctification is the observed process and state of having Jesus in us effectually. We start to resemble him objectively.

Saved. It is the happy state of those who obey Jesus as Lord. He is the Savior of all, but unfortunately not the Lord of all. Those saved are not subject to the penalties of the second judgment.

Sin. Sin is the inner disposition of independence and rebellion that was first manifested in Adam, wherein he decided what was right and wrong without reference to God's manifest will and commandment. Sin has both positive and negative aspects. By right, Satan assigns a positive Sin disposition to all humans at birth. Negatively, it is an absence of grace; our spirit lies fallow (Luke 4:6). If the conception of Christ without a human father is any indication, it can be argued that Sin comes through the human father.

Sinner's Prayer. The sinner's prayer is a shibboleth for evangelical Christians who have elevated it to the status of a sacrament. The prayer typically leads the person praying to "accept" Jesus as Savior. Elements critical to any prayer purporting to change God's attitude toward a sinner are:

1. An acknowledgement of a Sin heredity and responsibility for actual sins.
2. Thanksgiving for Christ's sacrifice on the Cross which has justified the sinner without qualification.
3. A confession of powerlessness to reform.
4. An unconditional ceding of the person's will to God in all matters.
5. An invitation to the Holy Spirit to come to the sinner without limit or constraint that the living Jesus might reign in their heart as Lord (Ps 51:17; Luke 23:40–43).

Such a prayer needs to be repeated by a Christian on a regular basis, preferably in the context of public worship. These critical elements are subsumed in the "Confession of Sin" and "Prayer of Humble Access" in the 1928 *Book of Common Prayer*.

Sins. These are the actual acts of rebellion performed by humans under the influence of a Sin disposition. They are indicators of a deeper spiritual malady. All sins are covered by the blood of Christ.

Synergistic. In the case of soteriology, synergism refers to developments that involve both God and man. God's call to his children is monergistic, our response to that call is synergistic, in that it can be resisted or ignored if we so choose.

Worship. People are by nature servants, and we confer worship to the extent we obey God or other gods. When we obey the Devil or his minions, we worship amiss, and we are degraded in our thinking and our behavior. When we obey God, we worship properly and are granted increased intellectual understanding, spiritual perception, and behavioral holiness.

Wrath. Wrath is a present and future enmity on the part of God towards people who grieve the Holy Spirit, who do not have the life of Christ in them, and who thereby prove fruitless. That God sacrificed his son for the sins of the world is of no import to such people.

Bibliography

Allen, Robert S. *Lucky Forward: The History of General George Patton's Third U.S. Army.* New York: McFadden, 1947.

Arminius, James. "Analysis of the Ninth Chapter of St. Paul's Epistle to the Romans, addressed to Gellius Snecanus." In *The Works of James Arminius* 3, 485–519. Grand Rapids: Baker, 1986.

Bailey, Robert Arthur. "God's Good News to the Romans." https://www.inthebeginning.org/structure/romans.pdf.

Bible Hub. "Romans 5:5." Interlinear Exposition. https://biblehub.com/interlinear/romans/5-5.htm.

Bloesch, Donald. *God, Authority & Salvation.* Essentials of Evangelical Theology 1. San Francisco: Harper & Row, 1978.

Brown, Lesley, ed. *The New Shorter Oxford English Dictionary* 2. Oxford: Clarendon, 1993.

Calder, Frederick. *Memoirs of Simon Episcopius.* London: Hayward and Moore, 1838.

Calvin, John. *Commentaries on the Epistle of Paul the Apostle to the Romans.* Translated and edited by John Owen. Edinburgh: Calvin Translation Society , 1849.

———. *Institutes of the Christian Religion in Two Volumes.* Translated by Ford Lewis Battles. Westminster: Philadelphia, 1960.

Chambers, Oswald. *My Utmost for His Highest.* New York: Dodd, Mead, 1935.

Durant, Will. *The Reformation: A History of European Civilization from Wyclif to Calvin: 1300–1564.* The Story of Civilization 4. New York: Simon and Schuster, 1957.

———. *The Story of Philosophy.* New York: Washington Square, 1952.

Freud, Sigmund. "Historical Notes: A Letter From Freud." American Journal of Psychiatry 107, 10 (1951) 786–787.

Kittelson, James. *Luther the Reformer.* Minneapolis, MN: Augsburg, 1986.

Lewis, C. S. "Priestesses in the Church?" In *God in the Dock*, Grand Rapids: William B. Eerdmans, 1970.

Lloyd-Jones, D. Martyn. *Romans*, 6 vols. Grand Rapids: Zondervan, 1970.

Luther, Martin. *Commentary on the Epistle to the Galatians.* Grand Rapids: Zondervan, 1967.

———.*Career of the Reformer IV.* Luther's Works 34. Edited by Lewis William Spitz. St. Louis: Concordia, 1960.

———. *Preface to the Letter of St. Paul to the Romans by Martin Luther.* Translated by Bro. Andrew Thornton, 1983. https://www.ccel.org/l/luther/romans/pref_romans.html.

———. *Sermons of Martin Luther* 3. Grand Rapids: Baker, 1983.

Meinardus, Otto F. A. "Paul's Missionary Journey to Spain: Tradition and Folklore." *The Biblical Archaeologist* 41 (June 1978) 61–63.

Meissner, Alfred. *Heinrich Heine: Erinnerungen*. Hamburg: Hoffmann and Campe, 1858.

Nestle, Eberhard, et al. *Novum Testamentum Graece*. 27th ed. Stuttgart: Deutsche Bibelgesellschaft, 1993.

Packer, J. I. "Let's Stop Making Women Presbyters." *Christianity Today*. Wheaton: Christianity Today International, February 11, 1991.

Pascal, Blaise. *Pensées*. New York: Penguin Books, 1966.

Schaeffer, Francis. "The Universe and Two Chairs," In *Death in the City*, The Complete Works of Francis A. Schaeffer, Volume Four: A Christian View of the Church. Westchester, IL: Crossway Books, 1982.

Society For Propagating The Gospel Among The Indians And Others In North-America. *Brief account of the Society for Propagating the Gospel among the Indians and Others in North America*. Boston, 1798. https://www.loc.gov/item/00515719/

The Congregationalist and Christian world. Boston: Pilgrim, 1915.

www.ingramcontent.com/pod-product-compliance
Lightning Source LLC
LaVergne TN
LVHW050645100826
845148LV00011B/1993

* 9 7 8 1 7 2 5 2 7 3 9 3 1 *